Fortress • 60

The Forts of the Meuse in World War I

Clayton Donnell • Illustrated by H Johnson, L Ray & B Delf

Series editors Marcus Cowper and Nikolai Bogdanovic

First published in Great Britain in 2007 by Osprey Publishing,
Midland House, West Way, Botley, Oxford OX2 0PH, UK
443 Park Avenue South, New York, NY 10016, USA
E-mail: info@ospreypublishing.com

A CIP catalogue record for this book is available from the British Library

ISBN: 978 1 84603 114 4

Page layout by Ken Vail Graphic Design, Cambridge, UK
Typeset in Monotype Gill Sans and ITC Stone Serif
Maps by The Map Studio Ltd
Index by Alison Worthington
Originated by United Graphics, Singapore
Printed in China through Bookbuilders

07 08 09 10 11   10 9 8 7 6 5 4 3 2 1

For a catalogue of all books published by Osprey Military and Aviation please contact:

NORTH AMERICA
Osprey Direct, c/o Random House Distribution Center, 400 Hahn Road,
Westminster, MD 21157
E-mail: info@ospreydirect.com

ALL OTHER REGIONS
Osprey Direct UK, P.O. Box 140 Wellingborough, Northants, NN8 2FA, UK
E-mail: info@ospreydirect.co.uk

www.ospreypublishing.com

Acknowledgments

My heartfelt thanks to the following. To Colonel Yves
Deraymaeker of the Musée du Génie, Jambes (Namur) for
his invaluable assistance during my visit, and to Colonel André
Laurent for his time and knowledge. Many thanks to Robert
Britte and Emile Coenen of the Centre Liègois d'Histoire et
d'Architecture Militaire for the images and information they
provided. Also at Liège, to Sylvain Vanderwalle of the Fort de
Loncin for our very thorough visit there; to Daniel Bastin for
his hospitality at the Fort de Hollogne; and to Roger Weeckmans
of the Fort de Barchon. Thanks to Dan, Robin and Mark for your
company and photos, to Johan, Hans and Vincent for your
company, and to Amelia for your help with the video.
Final thanks to M. Boijean and M. Bracke of the archives
of the Musée Royale de l'Armée at Brussels.

The Fortress Study Group (FSG)

The object of the FSG is to advance the education of the public
in the study of all aspects of fortifications and their armaments,
especially works constructed to mount or resist artillery. The FSG
holds an annual conference in September over a long weekend
with visits and evening lectures, an annual tour abroad lasting
about eight days, and an annual Members' Day.
The FSG journal *FORT* is published annually, and its newsletter
Casemate is published three times a year. Membership is
international. For further details, please contact:

The Secretary, c/o 6 Lanark Place, London, W9 1BS, UK

Contents

Introduction

At 0530hrs on 15 August 1914, 11 days after the German invasion of Belgium, a 1,600lb shell from a Krupp 42cm siege gun struck the powder magazine of Fort de Loncin, one of the 'forts of the Meuse' at Liège. From 4 August German troops had struggled to smash through the city's stubborn ring of forts, which kept them from sweeping across the Belgian plain into France. The giant siege guns had been carried piece by piece to the battlefield after it was determined that the only way to get through the fortress barrier was to destroy the forts one by one. Fort de Loncin had been pounded steadily since the previous day. The garrison still refused to surrender, but this particular shell reached the magazine filled with 12 tons of powder, and the ensuing explosion destroyed most of the fort's central redoubt, killing 250 Belgian soldiers and nearly killing General Gérard Leman, commander of the fortress of Liège. The resistance at Loncin ended. The following day the last two forts surrendered and the road to Paris was open at last.

General Brialmont's statue on the Rue Brialmont in Brussels. (Colonel Yves Deraymaeker)

In 1891 the forts of the Meuse, the crowning works of Belgian Army Engineer General Henri Alexis Brialmont, were the marvel of modern military engineering and the result of significant improvements in military technology since the middle of the century. Like his European counterparts, Brialmont had recognized the changes that were needed to keep permanent fortification technology in step with developments in the artillery that would be used against it. In 1850, little had changed in fortress building since the time of Vauban, France's great fortress builder. Many of Europe's major cities were still ringed by bastioned fortifications built to withstand sieges. The last formal siege using sap, parallel and smoothbore cannon took place at Antwerp in 1832. French howitzers and mortars turned the central part of the fortress to rubble. The bastion, built to withstand low-angle fire, had become useless. The Germans developed the 'polygonal' system in which caponiers replaced the bastion and provided flanking protection for the ditch.

The 1870s witnessed the arrival of 'rifled' artillery; smooth-bore tubes were replaced by tubes with spiralling grooves cast into the inner surface of the barrels, which caused the shell to spin and improved its range and accuracy. Artillery batteries could now fire from a greater distance and cause greater damage while being relatively safe from counter-battery fire. At Poznan in Poland the Germans built a ring of forts that stretched further and further into the countryside to keep the city safe from the ever-improving range of artillery. Thus, in a short period of time, the style of fortifications shifted from bastioned curtain walls to detached polygonal ring forts. Artillery caused this change in style, but further developments in the 1880s also caused a change in form.

4

In 1883 Melinite, a highly volatile compound of picric acid, was discovered and tested in high-explosive steel shells. Widely published tests were conducted in 1886 against France's declassified Fort de la Malmaison, causing great damage to the masonry structures. In May 1887 the French built special 1.5m-thick concrete casemates that proved to be significantly more durable. From that point on, forts throughout Europe would be built using concrete. Some concrete elements already existed, such as protective collars around gun turrets, and as facing on the walls of casemates. General Brialmont was the first to use it as the main ingredient. His forts of the Meuse were the first to be built entirely of concrete and steel.

Improved field artillery changed the structure of forts while naval developments would change the nature of fortress artillery. In 1855 ironclad ships were used for the first time in the Crimean War. Their success against bombardment from coastal forts led to the development of iron and steel armour plating for land-based fortifications. The revolving turret was also developed from naval guns. In the 1850s the Bessemer Steel process was developed to refine iron into a form of steel that was more pure and could be shaped more easily. Renowned military engineers like Gruson developed a cast-iron, revolving turret with curved sections to deflect shot. Schumann improved on the Gruson design with a retractable turret and a 21cm short-barrelled cannon in a turret built flush to the ground. Mougin took the turret one step further designing his 'Fort de l'Avenir' in 1886 – a concrete monolith built into the ground with guns in steel turrets. A prototype was built at Verdun's Froideterre in 1887, and the design was used in Germany's East and West Forts at Mutzig. The age of concrete and steel had arrived.

Brialmont's forts of the Meuse were the best example of the new design. They would be made of concrete strong enough to withstand 21cm shells, the most powerful guns in existence at the time and the largest mobile enough to be a

Mougin's 'Fort de l'Avenir'. Note the guns massed in a concrete bloc in the centre, very similar to Brialmont's central massif used in the forts of the Meuse. (Author's collection)

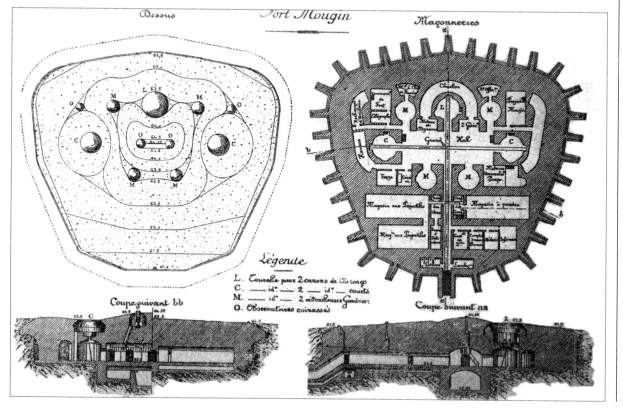

Construction in progress at Fort de Hollogne near Liège. (Royal Army Museum in Brussels, Belgium)

factor in a siege. The fort's guns would be protected in revolving steel turrets. Men and munitions would be housed in concrete underground shelters. Plans for the Liège and Namur bridgeheads were approved on 1 February 1887 and construction began the following summer. On 29 October 1891 the new forts were turned over to the Belgian Army.

The three-year project would cost 71.6 million Belgian francs and require a crew of over 9,000 workers to move millions of cubic metres of dirt, pour millions of cubic metres of concrete and install dozens of guns in armoured steel turrets. Twenty-one modern forts were built around the cities of Liège and Namur to defend the strategic rail, river and road arteries that followed the Meuse River valley and passed through a narrow gap to the flat, open plain of Flanders. Although they were the most modern forts of their time, they would be severely tested in the opening battles of World War I. Sadly, they were already obsolete by then, and their weaknesses would be revealed in short order.

Chronology

1815	The Congress of Vienna establishes the Kingdom of the Netherlands, comprised of the former republics of Holland and Belgium, with William I of Orange as king.
25 August 1830	Belgian rebellion against the Dutch monarchy begins in Brussels.
4 October 1830	Belgian Declaration of Independence.
December 1830	London Conference recognizes independent Kingdom of Belgium; civil war with the Netherlands continues.
1839	Dutch–Belgian Peace Treaty signed, granting Dutch recognition of Belgian independence and guarantee of 'perpetual Belgian neutrality' by the major European powers.
1851	King Leopold I creates a commission to study the defensive system of Belgium from a neutral point of view.
1860	General Henri Alexis Brialmont, Belgian Army Engineer, builds eight polygonal forts around Antwerp.
September 1870	Franco-Prussian War threatens to spill over into Belgian territory. Great Britain threatens intervention on the side of Belgium against any power that violates Belgium's neutrality.
1882	General Brialmont publishes his treatise entitled *Situation Militaire de la Belgique*, and proposes the creation of a ring of forts around Liège and Namur.
1 June 1887	Belgian Parliament approves 24 million francs for the construction of 21 of Brialmont's forts of the Meuse.
28 July 1888	Groundbreaking begins.
29 October 1891	The forts are formally turned over to the Belgian Army.
1905	Count von Schlieffen, Chief of Staff of the German Imperial Army, publishes his 'memorandum' recommending an attack on France through Belgium and Holland. His successor, Moltke, amends the memo to exclude a violation of Dutch neutrality.
28 June 1914	Archduke Franz Ferdinand of Austria, heir to the throne, is assassinated in Sarajevo, Bosnia, setting off a diplomatic furore throughout Europe that will lead to total war.
2 August 1914	Germany delivers an ultimatum to Belgium to allow German troops to pass through Belgium to fight the French or risk war and occupation. King Albert refuses.
2–4 August 1914	German troops of the Army of the Meuse under General von Emmich, vanguard of the German main force, invade Belgium near Aachen.
5–6 August 1914	German troops suffer heavy casualties during direct assault on the Belgian fortified positions at Liège. The Germans infiltrate between the forts into the city. General Leman, commander of Belgian forces, withdraws the army, leaving the forts to fight on their own.
8–16 August 1914	Heavy German siege guns ceaselessly bombard the 12 forts of Liège, and they surrender one by one.
18–23 August 1914	German forces attack the fortified position of Namur, avoiding direct assaults on the forts, attacking the intervals instead and shelling the forts. A similar scenario to Liège develops and the forts surrender.
1914–15	The forts of the Meuse are abandoned.

Design and development

In 1888, outdated bastioned fortresses were the only fortifications existing at Liège and Namur. The citadel and Fort de la Chartreuse overlooked Liège, whilst Namur's citadel was one of the largest in Europe though it was useless against an attack by a modern army using modern artillery.

In his treatise *Situation Militaire de la Belgique*, written in 1882, Brialmont made the case that it was inevitable that France and Germany would again go to war. When they did they would choose the most likely invasion route into either country, the Meuse Valley. The Vosges Mountains and General Séré de Rivières' powerful fortress line that extended from Switzerland to Maubeuge blocked Alsace and Lorraine and the most vulnerable sector of the French frontier was a 60km front between Dun and Mezières. In order to concentrate its forces against this front, Germany would need to use rail lines that ran through Luxembourg and Belgium, causing them to violate the neutrality of those countries. A French invasion of Germany would also avoid an attack through Alsace and Lorraine and the French Army would most likely march on the undefended Sambre and Oise Valleys into Belgium towards Namur, and subsequently down the Meuse Valley. It was therefore essential that the line of the Meuse be defended. Both Liège and Namur were the keys to Belgium, through which ran a vast network of railways and roads.

In addition to the Meuse Valley, the German General Staff, Count Alfred von Schlieffen in particular, noted the great value of the flat plains to the west of Liège. They formed a natural pathway from Eastern and Central Europe through which a large army could sweep around behind the French forces concentrated in Alsace and Lorraine. Militarily the Belgian plain of Flanders presented four prime advantages to the attacker: there was no interruption by a topographical barrier of any great importance; it was supplied by a dense network of roads and railways on which to move troops and supplies; the land was productive enough to supply food for long periods of time; it passed close to coal and iron deposits near the Ardennes. Flanders was the perfect gateway to Northern France. In 1906, General Helmuth von Moltke, Chief of the German General Staff, stated:

> Liège and Namur are of no importance in themselves. They would be weakly garrisoned but they were strong places. They block the Meuse railway, whose use during the war cannot therefore be counted upon. It is of the greatest importance to take at least Liège at an early stage, in order to have the railway in one's hands. The possession of Liège is the [absolute essential] of our advance.

To the French or German invader, Liège was the 'gateway to Belgium', perhaps even the 'key to Paris or Berlin'. The city had three train terminals, seven rail lines, 17 roads passing through it and 12 bridges across the Meuse River. To the north-east lies the Plateau of Hervé, while to the south-east is the heavily wooded Ardennes Forest with its deep valleys, difficult territory for an army to attack through. To the north and west lies the Plain of Hesbaye. The ramparts of the heights of the right and left banks of the Meuse overlook these features. The target for any enemy attack would be the 16km gap between Liège and the Dutch border (see the map on page 34).

To the south-west, Namur guarded five railway lines and its main station connected Brussels, Luxembourg, Liège, Charleroi, Tirlemont, Givet and Dinant.

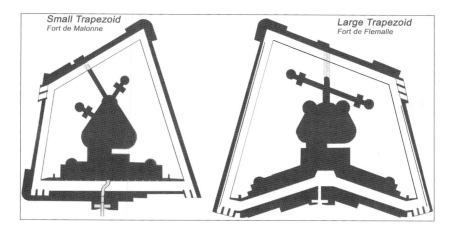

Small Trapezoid
Fort de Malonne

Large Trapezoid
Fort de Flemalle

A comparison of the large and small trapezoidal forts. Note the rectilinear and bastioned traces of the gorge front. The central massif of the large fort had an additional 21cm gun turret. (Author's collection)

It also had bridges over the Meuse and the Sambre. Brialmont's treatise made a favourable impression on the army and, with the help of some influential defence ministry officials, the project was approved.

Brialmont's construction plans were more far reaching than final funding would allow and he was forced to economize. The law of 1 June 1887 allotted 24 million francs to the project even before geological studies had been completed. The final allocation was 71.6 million francs. Brialmont was furious that he had not been given more funding and declared that the government would one day regret being so frugal, in particular for not allowing him the funds to build a fort at Visé, where German cavalry would easily cross the Meuse on 4 August 1914.

Brialmont's designs were simple and economical. The forts were either triangular or trapezoidal, depending on the terrain. He chose the triangular trace to reduce the number of flanking features needed, and to adapt the trace more easily to the terrain. The trapezoidal trace fitted more easily on narrower tracts of land. The forts of the Meuse were the first forts built in modules with standardized construction. There were only three sets of designs for the gorge ditch, plus two each for the central massif, connecting gallery to the head casemate and the head casemate. Each element was chosen based on its mission and location (see the diagram on page 32).

Brialmont's forts were also the first to be built entirely of concrete, a mix of the compound cement with sand, stones, and water. Portland cement, invented in 1824, was the most common cement compound used in both concrete and mortar. The concrete was not reinforced with metal rods, as this was an innovation of the mid-1890s.

Concrete type	Location used	Mix	Volume of each mix per m³
1	Foundations, footings, abutments, foundation walls	Cement – 1 part; sand/gravel* – 3.6 parts; pebbles – 6.3 parts	143 litres; 660 litres; 900 litres
2	Vaults, exposed masonry	Cement – 1 part; sand/gravel* – 2.6 parts; pebbles – 3.6 parts	250 litres; 660 litres; 900 litres
*Contained ²/₃ rough sand, ¹/₃ fine sand from the Meuse River			

In May 1888 The Belgian government invited contractors to bid on the project and, on 1 July 1888, the project was awarded to a French firm, Hallier, Letellier Brothers and Jules Barratoux. Their headquarters was set up at Liège and, on 28 July 1888, groundbreaking began on a project that would take 30 months to complete and would include the excavation of building sites, removal of trees and earth, and construction of casernes, galleries, gun turret wells, ditches, revetments, retaining walls, wells, cisterns, drainage, sewers, aqueducts, access

Construction of the forts of the Meuse

This shows the stages of construction of the right gorge front. In reality, the forts were not built in this way. The entire building would be in the same stage of construction. This is a representation to condense those stages. The background shows the finished postern entry and the left counterscarp caserne. Cement was mixed in the building on the glacis overlooking the gorge ditch. Concrete was mixed inside and poured down a chute into wagons below the front platform. It was taken on wagons to the location of the pouring.

roads and military roads, plus the finishing work of floors and stairs, wood trim, doors, fittings and plumbing.

Engineers built 60km of roads at Liège and 40km at Namur, plus 100km of new railway lines called the 'Strategic Road'. Sixty large and 75 small locomotives, and 2,000 wagons were used to haul materials along these rail lines.

A magnificent sketch of the construction logistics at Fort de Barchon. The plan shows the construction and support buildings with the fort in the centre. Rail lines delivered supplies to the site. This is one of a set of 12 prints found in the trash by the Centre Liègois d'Histoire et d'Architecture Militaire. (Centre Liègois d'Histoire et d'Architecture Militaire at Liège, Belgium)

Sectors	Earthworks (m³)	Concrete (m³)	Brick (m³)	Mortar coatings (m²)	Surfaces of mortar (m²)
Liège – L Bank	775,000	295,740	4,920	164,500	21,150
Liège – R Bank	705,000	305,400	7,800	171,200	21,180
Namur – L Bank	820,000	328,000	6,130	195,760	20,180
Namur – R Bank	420,000	145,000	2,758	76,000	9,300
Total	2,720,000	1,074,140	21,608	607,460	71,840

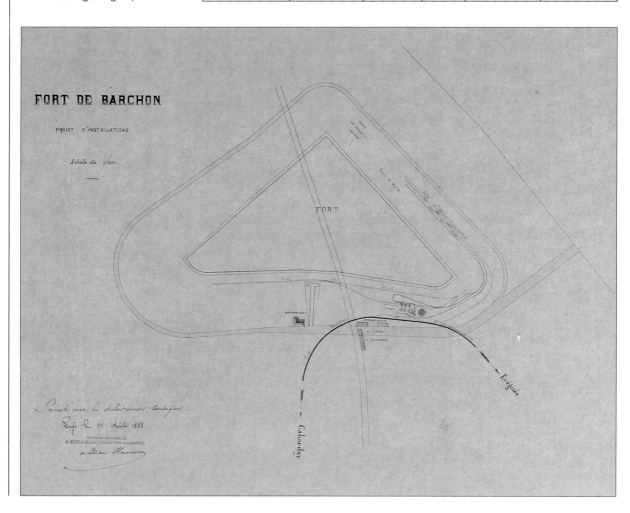

FORT DE BARCHON

PROJET D'INSTALLATIONS

Echelle de 1/1250.

FORT

Construction of the forts of the Meuse

Fort de Liers in 1890, showing the service bridge and the addition of wooden framework on the eastern face of the counterscarp wall. These photos are from a collection of five albums presented to Gen. Brialmont after the completion of construction. (Royal Army Museum in Brussels, Belgium)

A number of methods were used to move raw materials to the construction sites. Sand and stone were dredged from the local rivers and transported by inclined plane or aerial tramway to the manufacturing plants at each fort where the cement would be mixed into concrete. Roads, gravel- and sand-dredging facilities and cement factories were built in the vicinity of each construction site. Each fort had its own concrete and mortar fabrication installations located on the crest overlooking the gorge ditch. Concrete was mixed at the concrete fabrication plant, placed into wagons, and transported over small-gauge railway tracks or handcarts to where it was poured. Warehouses close to the cement factory and next to the delivery routes could store an eight-day supply of cement. Smaller warehouses were used to store oil and grease for the machinery, as well as 15,000m^3 of sand and gravel supplies, and to provide workspace for blacksmiths and cartwrights. Water was pumped from the rivers or from underground wells into masonry reservoirs and used for a variety of purposes.

Some materials were manufactured at other locations and transported by rail to the building sites. 300,000 tons of Portland cement were manufactured at two cement plants in France and three in Belgium. Wood was cut from both foreign and Belgian forests. Bricks were cast at each site. Quarries in the Ourthe Valley provided stone tiles for stairs and floors.

Once all of the logistical pieces were in place, construction could begin. In the first 15 months 100,000 to 175,000m^3 of dirt were excavated to prepare the foundations of each fort. The ground was levelled and foundation trenches were dug. Wood was then used to build frames in which to pour the concrete for each of the forts' elements. Layers of concrete were poured, a little at a time, until the walls reached the required height, then vaulted ceilings were poured over the top. The shape of the ceilings for each chamber or gallery was formed with curved wooden frames. Concrete was poured over the top, once again in layers, until it reached the required thickness. The contract called for the framework to be left in place to allow the concrete to dry for 15 days (20 in winter). This was later reduced to four days for footings and eight days for vaulting. After the concrete had dried and the wooden frames were removed, mortar was spread to smooth the surface and fill in any holes. It was then brushed with a stiff brush. In certain structures, like the postern entry and the counterscarp and gorge front casernes, earth was placed over the top to create an additional layer of protection. The thickness of the concrete for the walls and ceilings depended on

Pouring of concrete on the gorge front caserne at Embourg in 1890. (Royal Army Museum in Brussels, Belgium)

the vulnerability of the structure to be protected. The walls of the gorge front caserne were 1.5m thick, the top of the central massif 4m thick.

Concrete was often poured and then left to dry overnight because crews did not have the illumination to work at night. This created a problem because the next layer was not poured until the following morning. Often, by this time, the previous layer had dried and proper bonding didn't take place. The results were evident at Fort de Loncin, where, during the final explosion, different layers that had not properly bonded lifted off of each other then settled again, causing severe structural damage.

The forts were armed with a variety of long- and short-range weapons. The approaches to the fort were defended by Nordenfeld 5.7cm rapid-fire guns housed in steel turrets and casemates. Long-range 12, 15 and 21cm guns were manufactured by Krupp and housed in armoured steel turrets. These were built by a number of French, Belgian and German manufacturers. Belgian factories built some of the turret components but not the entire piece. The total cost of 171 turrets was 26 million francs, plus 3 million francs for testing, transportation and mounting.

A spectacular view of the central massif of Fort de Boncelles. The interior postern entry is visible in the centre. The central massif is visible above the terraced earth. (Royal Army Museum in Brussels, Belgium)

A Nordenfeld 5.7cm rapid-fire gun, like those found in the forts of the Meuse. This one was restored by the Ateliers FAB and now resides in the museum of Fort de Loncin. (Author's collection)

The Nordenfeld 5.7cm rapid-fire gun carriage in the right gorge casemate at Fort de Loncin. Note the cracks in the wall from the final explosion that destroyed the fort. (Author's collection)

Turrets were made mostly of steel. The floors of the gun chambers and intermediate levels were made of wood planks over steel frames. They were delivered to the forts and placed into wells cast into the concrete massif or the salient angles of the central redoubt. Additional protection for the turret was provided by 'advanced armour', a protective steel collar that encircled the turret well and prevented the turret from being dislodged if the concrete was damaged.

All of the turrets rotated through 360 degrees. The 5.7cm rapid-fire gun and the searchlight turret were retractable and the gun and searchlight could be hidden below the level of the advanced armour. This was not so with the big guns and the mouths of the gun barrels were constantly exposed in the top of the cap.

The 5.7cm turret rested on a cylindrical column that moved up and down inside a sleeve. A counterbalance on the end of the column eased the manual raising and lowering of the turret. The turret was raised 60cm and the cannon was moved forward for firing. The turret's Nordenfeld gun fired at a rate of 20 shots per minute.

The forts' guns were manufactured separately from the turrets and they were housed in the gun chamber of each turret, which was an armoured cylinder. It rested on rollers that moved along tracks on a shelf around the circumference of the well. The turret was moved, aimed and fired by a series of wheels and ratchets located in the middle and lower levels. The turret could be rotated quickly or more slowly for precise aim. A turret was aimed directly by an observer looking through a small visor, or indirectly using a graduated ring that showed directional headings in $\frac{1}{20}$ths of a degree. In some of the guns the aiming ring was in the intermediate level and an artilleryman communicated the headings by acoustic tube to the gun commander. In Brialmont's specifications

The turret cap rests on the advanced armour. This damaged turret is located at Fort de Loncin. (Author's collection)

to the engineers, he stated it should take 1½ minutes to make a complete revolution of the gun, and three revolutions in five minutes. The vertical angle of the guns could also be adjusted to increase or decrease range. It should take one minute to move the gun from the limit of one angle of its range to the other limit. Once the proper angle was reached a brake was engaged to keep the gun in position.

Each turret had a manually operated elevator to hoist the charge and the projectile in a metal basket from the lower level to the gun chamber. A chain ran in a loop around the outside of the hoist frame and one man could pull the basket up to the gun chamber near the breech. To keep out gas fumes from enemy shells, as well as to expel fumes from the guns, a hand-operated ventilator was used to place the turret under negative pressure. Each cannon was equipped with a hydraulic recoil brake filled with 80 per cent glycerine and 20 per cent water. In case of a malfunction, a gun could be changed for another in as little as three hours.

Type of gun	Number in large forts	Number in small forts	Manufacturer of turret	Cost
2 x 15cm cannon	1	0	Gruson, St Chamond, Creusot, *Vanderkerhove	290,000 F
2 x 12cm cannon	2	0	Chatillon-Commentry	231,500 F
1 x 12cm cannon	0	2	Chatillon-Commentry, Ateliers de la Meuse, **Marcinelle-Couillet	195,000 F
1 x 21cm howitzer	2	1	Gruson	112,000 F
1 x 5.7cm gun in turret	4	3	Gruson	106,500 F
1 x 5.7cm gun in casemate	9	9	N/A	N/A
Searchlight	1	1	Ateliers de la Meuse	70,000 F

* Only at Liège

** The large forts of Namur and Fort Boncelles at Liège were equipped with two 12cm turrets fabricated by Chatillon-Commentry and Marcinelle-Couillet. Chatillon-Commentry and Ateliers de la Meuse built the remaining 12cm turrets of Liège.

5.7cm Nordenfeld casemate model cannons were mounted on cone-shaped, wheeled gun carriages. In the large forts, two guns were located in each casemate of the gorge front (four total), four in the head casemate, and one in the casemate defending the entry ramp. In the large trapezoidal forts, two guns were placed in the supplementary casemate that defended the fourth angle. Mobile 5.7cm cannons, used by infantry troops, were kept in garages along the counterscarp wall.

In the small forts, four 5.7cm Nordenfeld cannons were located in two casemates in the centre of the gorge ditch in the re-entrant angle, or two in the lateral flanking coffer if the gorge was rectilinear. One 5.7cm defended the access ramp and four were placed in the head casemate (two in the supplementary flanking casemate in the trapezoidal forts).

Description of the guns									
Type of gun	Diameter of turret	Angle of fire (degrees)	Barrel length	Weight of turret	Number of crew	Projectile types used	Range	Manufacturer
15cm M.1886	4.8m	+25 to -2	3.7m	224 tons	25 on three levels	Iron, steel, shrapnel, pellets	8.5km	Krupp
12cm M.1889	4.8m	+25 to -3	3m	188 tons	25 on three levels	Same as 15cm	8km	Krupp
21cm M.1889 + 1891	3.6m	+ 35 to -5	2.5m	100 tons	13 on two levels	Iron, steel, shrapnel, pellets	6.9km curved	Krupp
5.7cm M.1888	2.1m	+ 10 to -8	1.5m	34 tons	six on two levels	Canister w/pellets	300m	*Nordenfeld

* 5.7cm in casemate manufactured by Cockerill-Krupp

Munitions for the 5.7cm turrets were stored fully charged (with primer, fuse and charge) in chambers under the turrets or in the casemates. A small number of shells were stored in racks in the space under the advanced armour inside the gun chamber. Elements for the larger guns were stocked separately. The 12, 15 and 21cm shells did not have cartridge cases. The projectile and the propellant charge were loaded separately, with the projectile inserted first and then the propellant charge. Shells were stored in the munitions magazines at the foot of the turrets. The propellant charges were loaded in silk sacs and stored on tables

A steam-driven motor identical to those installed in the forts of the Meuse. This piece, and the one that follows, were installed for testing in the Fonderie Royale des Canons at Liège, and were used to train machinists and electricians. (Centre Liègois d'Histoire et d'Architecture Militaire at Liège, Belgium)

in the large powder magazines. The guns used black powder that produced a great deal of smoke and tended to obstruct observation. Smokeless powder was not available in 1891 and the guns were never modified.

The forts were equipped with the most modern machinery available at the time and affordable under the authorized budget. Power generation consisted of three elements – the steam engine, motor and dynamo. Each fort had a coal-fired steam boiler manufactured by de Naeyer in the lower level of the central massif. It was built with military requirements in mind and was reliable, lightweight, easily transportable, easily maintained and had quick vaporization pressure build up. Steam was pumped at high pressure through pipes into a single-cylinder, 20CV motor located on the floor above. The motor rotated a drive belt that was attached to a small dynamo. Copper wires in the dynamo revolved at 700rpm around a magnet, generating 154 amps of electricity at 80 volts. This powered the searchlight and its turret, lamps in the gun turret chambers, and water pumps for the well. Due to budgetary constraints, petrol lamps or miner's lamps were used to light the other combat posts. During an attack they often broke or were extinguished, plunging the interior into darkness and severely affecting the morale of the combatants. Eighty tons of coal were kept in storage for the large forts, slightly less for the smaller forts. Approximately 3,500 litres of petrol were stored at each fort for portable lamps.

Each fort had a large, 60cm-diameter searchlight with a powerful beam that could illuminate the surrounding area 2 to 3km away on a clear night. It was manufactured by Bouckaert & Shuckert Cie. and used arc technology to pass electrical current between carbon rods. The brightness could be adjusted by moving the rods closer together or farther apart, affecting the intensity of the electric spark. This was remarkable because at this time most of the world was still lit by gas, kerosene or candlepower. The searchlight was housed in an armoured turret built by the firm Ateliers de la Meuse at Sclessin near Liège. The thickness of the turret's vertical steel was 10cm and the cap 20cm of moulded steel. The searchlight lit the battlefield and could be used to send optical signals to adjacent forts if other forms of communication were cut. During the day the searchlight turret served as an observatory.

The business end of the electrical generation system. This is the dynamo that produced the electricity. A belt from the steam motor turned the magnet in the centre, producing 154 amps of power at 700rpm. (Centre Liègois d'Histoire et d'Architecture Militaire at Liège, Belgium)

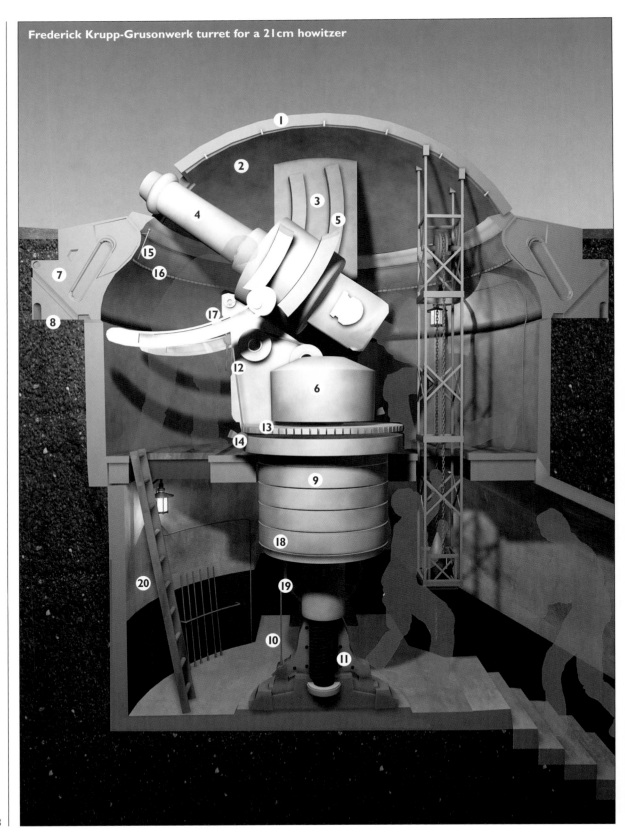

The bakery at Fort de Loncin. The dough-mixing machine is in the foreground and the oven behind it. Note the ventilation duct along the wall to the right, in existence only at Loncin. (Robin Ware)

The primary means of communication were telegraph or telephone over above-ground wires, extremely vulnerable to enemy damage or sabotage. The telephone was connected to a central station in the city manned by a civilian operator. The forts' commanders could not talk directly to one another unless the civilian operator connected them. All communications with forward observers and fire control were by telephone with direct observation lacking. Permanent observation posts were not constructed and commanders relied heavily on forward observers located in buildings or church steeples.

Latrines were sparse and poorly planned. The primary cause of the surrender of many of the forts was unbreathable, putrid air, with the main culprit being the inability, during wartime, to dispose of human waste. Even worse, with the exception of Fort de Loncin, latrines were located in the counterscarp, inaccessible in time of war after the troops were moved into the gorge front caserne and the central massif. Troops were forced to use makeshift latrines adjacent to the troop assembly room that, very simply, were insufficient to handle the volume, and produced terrible odours inside the enclosed, unventilated space.

With the exception, once again, of Fort de Loncin, which was equipped with an electrical ventilation system, the forts depended on natural ventilation through the windows or small vent shafts. In wartime, the forts were sealed up

Frederick Krupp-Grusonwerk turret for a 21cm howitzer

The turret is composed of a rounded steel cap (1), made of 20cm-thick cast iron between two plates of 2cm-thick steel. The cap rests on a steel frame (2) attached to two vertical steel plates (3) that make up the gun carriage. The howitzer (4) is affixed between the two plates and slides up or down along two grooves (5) on the inside of the carriage plates. The gun carriage is attached to a large flat bolt (6). These are the elements of the gun that rest and rotate on a shaft (9) in the centre of the turret. The gun carriage and turret cap, when they are not raised for firing, sit on four wedges of hardened cast iron (7) that are bolted together and that lie on a shelf (8) in the turret well. The shaft is raised by working a ratchet lever (10) at the base of the shaft that winds a screw (11) and forces

the shaft upwards. The howitzer is rotated to its firing coordinates slowly or rapidly. Slow rotation is accomplished by using another ratcheted lever (12) that engages the turning screw mechanism (13), or quickly by placing bars into four sockets (14) at the base of the gun carriage bolt and manually pushing the turret to the proper degree mark indicated by a pointer (15) on the directional indicator (16) encircling the turret. The gun is raised or lowered to its firing angle with a third level (17). The counterweight (18) below the floor balances the weight of the gun to ease the raising and lowering. It is attached to a steel cable that runs through a pulley system inside the carriage housing. Ventilation of the turret housing is assured by a manually operated ventilator located in an alcove (19) in the lower level. A ladder (20) provides access to the gun chamber.

as tight as a drum. Windows were secured by dropping steel rails horizontally into grooves that ran vertically along the concrete frame of the window. The steel rails were as wide as the opening and were laid, one on top of the other, until they completely covered the glass-paned window. A set of hinged armoured shutters attached to the outer wall, were closed over the top of the steel rails. Lack of ventilation added to the air quality problem. At Loncin, the ventilators stopped working when debris in the exhaust chimney shut down the motor.

The drainage system was poor and the forts were often damp and humid from the natural condensation of moisture on the roofs and walls. Rainwater drained from gutters on top of the central massif into the large cisterns built into the outside perimeter of the central massif. Water for drinking was pumped from underground wells into a reservoir adjacent to the well room. Rainwater or well water could reach a height of about 2m before it would run into a drain in the walls then into pipes that led to the casernes where it was used for drinking, bathing, washing and cooking, as well as to provide water for the steam engine. Water in the large cisterns was also designed to serve as 'liquid armour' protection for the central massif. However, during the bombardment at Liège some of the cisterns cracked, causing water to flood the barracks and the munitions storage rooms of some of the turrets. At Namur a metallic grid covered the outer walls of the cisterns for additional protection. In some forts, debris from the cisterns blocked the water pipes to the motors.

Troops were housed in rooms in the gorge front caserne. They slept in single rows of cots with eight, ten or 12 men to a room. Small wood stoves provided heat. In peacetime, the troops were housed in wooden barracks built on the glacis of the fort. These temporary barracks were burned down in time of war. The fort had no operating room, just a small infirmary in the gorge front caserne to extract bullets or shrapnel splinters.

Pantries, kitchens and bakeries were located in the counterscarp. Bread was baked on the premises and stored in racks in the bakery. Cattle were herded nearby and the fort's butcher kept a supply of meat available for the troops. In time of war, since the kitchens were closed, troops would be given prepared rations that included unleavened bread. Food stocks included a one-month stock of flour, biscuits for five days, dried meat for one month, sugar and small sweets for one month.

Tour of the sites

The forts of the Meuse were built on the heights around the cities of Namur and Liège. The top of the central massif might be visible from below or from a distance but, for the most part, the forts were invisible. From the perimeter of the fort the glacis sloped gently up to the ditch and was protected by wire entanglements. The combat zone of the fort was located across the ditch in the centre of the triangle or trapezoid. The head of the fort faced the enemy and the base was towards the city.

At the rear of the fort an access ramp 4m wide led from the military perimeter road down a 45-degree slope into the main entry, called the counterscarp postern. The access ramp was about 40m long and was typically paved with cobblestone. At the base of the ramp the ground levelled out into the entry drum, an enclosed killing ground defended by a casemate.

The rolling bridge at Fort de Hollogne. The wooden bridge rolled back into a space in the wall to the right, revealing an impassable pit. (Author's collection)

The crawlspace beneath the guardroom. From here the rolling bridge was moved in and out along the rails using the handgrips. (Robin Ware)

Postern entry – Fort de Hollogne, Liège

The entry portal was in the centre of the masking wall of the counterscarp postern. To the right and left of the entry portal tunnel were two large windows covered with iron grilles that looked out from two guardrooms on either side of the portal. The portal tunnel was 3m wide, 4m high and 14m long, and opened out at the far end into the gorge ditch. A wooden platform 5.75m long, called a rolling bridge, spanned the width of the access tunnel, and assured a passive defence of the entry ramp. The platform, built over a steel frame, had four wheels that moved on rails and resembled a railway flat car. The bridge could be pushed by hand in and out of a 1.5m-high crawlspace beneath one of the guardrooms, revealing a pit 4m deep.

Murder holes, or *meurtrières*, on each wall of the tunnel directly above the rolling bridge defended the tunnel opening. They could be closed off from inside of each guard chamber with metal shutters. On the other side of the rolling bridge was a decorative iron gate topped with spiked rails that could be locked to seal off the entry.

Inside the gate were doorways that led to the right and left to the gorge counterscarp caserne and the counterscarp postern entry guardrooms. One of the guardrooms had a trapdoor that led to the rolling bridge crawlspace and a staircase leading to the entry drum casemate. This casemate was 10m long and 3m wide. Along one wall were four rifle embrasures. A wooden platform 1.5m high was affixed to the wall just above the lower embrasures and allowed sentries to fire from the upper embrasures. The guardroom opposite doubled as a telegraph office.

The number of rooms in the gorge counterscarp caserne differed from fort to fort. Each fort had an office of the Chief of Artillery, a telegraph room, kitchen, pantry, laundry and washroom, jail cells in case of disciplinary problems,

TOP LEFT The very well preserved right guardroom at Fort de Loncin. In the corner is the trapdoor leading to the rolling bridge crawlspace beneath the floor. (Robin Ware)

TOP RIGHT An original wood-framed window overlooking the ditch. The grooves at the top of the windows allowed steel beams to be dropped into slots running parallel to the sides of the window, which protected them from shellfire. (Author's collection)

Postern entry – Fort de Hollogne, Liège

Brialmont placed the main entry to the Meuse forts in the rear. A road called the access ramp, flanked on either side by a steep embankment, led either up, or down to the postern entry. The entry portal led to the inner courtyard of the fort and gave access to offices, to the kitchen and bakery, the latrines and washrooms, and storage garages for mobile guns in the counterscarp. The entry had a moveable obstacle about 1m inside the portal called the *pont roulant*, or rolling bridge. Unlike the drawbridges used in castles or in the Séré de Rivières forts of France, this could be rolled away into a crawlspace under the right guardroom. When moved, it revealed a pit 4m deep. In the walls on either side of the pit were openings from the guardrooms called *meurtrières*, or 'murder holes', through which sentries could fire into the tunnel. The concrete on the roof of the fort was 2.5m thick. A layer of dirt 1.5m deep on the courtyard end of the tunnel and .5m deep on the entry side covered the concrete and provided an extra cushion of protection.

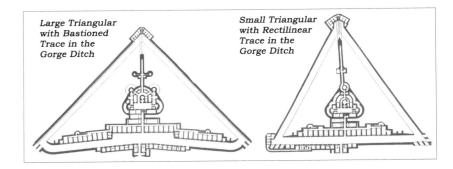

Large and small triangular forts. The gorge ditch on the left is bastioned. Guns in the right casemate fired towards Salient Angle I to the left. Guns in the left casemate fired towards Salient Angle III. The small fort has a rectilinear ditch and the flanking casemate is in Salient Angle III. (Author's collection)

Large Triangular with Bastioned Trace in the Gorge Ditch

Small Triangular with Rectilinear Trace in the Gorge Ditch

latrines, a munitions laboratory (to test fuses and powder) and garages for mobile cannons. Each room had a large wood-framed window with glass panes that looked out on the gorge ditch.

The walls of the counterscarp caserne adjacent to the ditch were 2.5m thick. The floors were paved with blue stone tiles and the walls were painted white with a tint of Prussian blue. Latrines consisted of either private stalls or water running down the wall into a gutter. Water for showers was piped into tanks in the ceiling of the washroom, and clothes were washed on horizontal stone tables built into the wall. Kitchens were provided with bake ovens and machines for churning bread dough, and bread was stored on wooden racks in the bakery. Additional food supplies were kept in a small pantry adjacent to the kitchen.

In most of the smaller forts a tunnel led from the counterscarp caserne to flanking casemates in the corner angle. These casemates were built on two levels and contained four chambers for 5.7cm guns, two on each floor. If the ditch became blocked by debris, the guns could be moved to the second level where they could fire over the blockage. Munitions for the guns were kept in storage rooms next to the gun chambers. Gun crews slept on portable cots in the casemate.

The gorge ditch ran either straight across the rear of the fort or at a slight angle from each corner of the base to the centre of the gorge front caserne. Where an angular base was used, pseudo-bastioned casemates flanked the opposite angle of the base. The casemate on the right of the entry fired across the entry and down to Salient Angle I. The casemate on the left covered the ditch from the entry to Salient Angle III. Each casemate had two gun chambers for 5.7cm guns on a single level.

The gorge front ditch at Fort de Loncin. The counterscarp is on the left, the central redoubt on the right. Here on 14 August 1914, Commandant Naessens assembled his troops to rally them for the fight to come. (Author's collection)

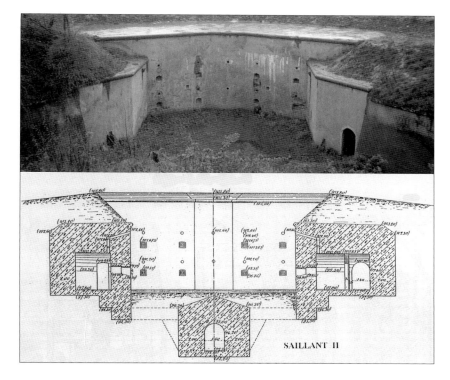

SAILLANT II

The head casemate of the fort provided flanking fire for the left and right laterals. The door showing on the right is the emergency exit that was sealed up. The gallery to the central massif runs underground. This is the head casemate at Fort de Hollogne. (Author's collection)

At the head of the fort was a casemate similar to the counterscarp flanking casemates. It had eight gun chambers for four 5.7cm guns on two levels, with munitions storage next to the gun chambers and a staircase leading to the upper level. The main access to the head casemate was an underground gallery that led from the central massif. If the gallery was blocked there was a hidden doorway in the masking wall of the lower level of the head casemate that opened into the ditch. It was sealed up and invisible from the outside. A set of tools left inside the sealed-up entrance could be used to break through the thin wall to the outside.

The gorge front caserne was built into the rear face of the central redoubt and ran nearly the whole length of the gorge front ditch and was connected by a hallway to the central massif. Rooms inside the gorge front caserne ran its length and each room had a large window open to the ditch. All of the windows in the rooms of the caserne opened onto the gorge front ditch and could be sealed with steel rails in the same manner as the counterscarp rooms. In most forts, from the centre to the right or left, the layout of the gorge front caserne was symmetrical.

The main entrance to the central redoubt, called the escarp postern, was located in the centre of the gorge front caserne, off centre so it could not be seen from the outside entry ramp. The escarp postern was identical in design and protection to the main entry. There are no known photos in existence of an original escarp postern entry. All were heavily damaged and modernized in one form or another after the battle with the exception of Fort de Loncin, which was destroyed completely.

Inside the gate was an intersection of three hallways. The central massif, powder magazines, steam engine and coal storage were straight ahead down the central gallery. To the right and left was a corridor that ran along the entire length of the gorge front caserne and perpendicular to the central gallery. Along this corridor were barracks rooms, an infirmary, armoury and mess facilities. Barracks rooms were separated from the hallway by a brick wall with a door in the centre and glass windows flanking the door.

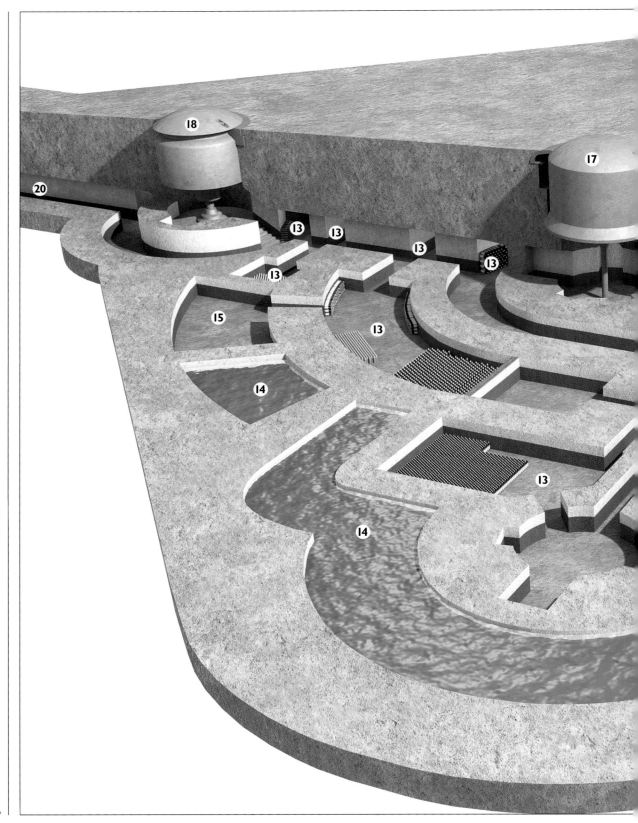

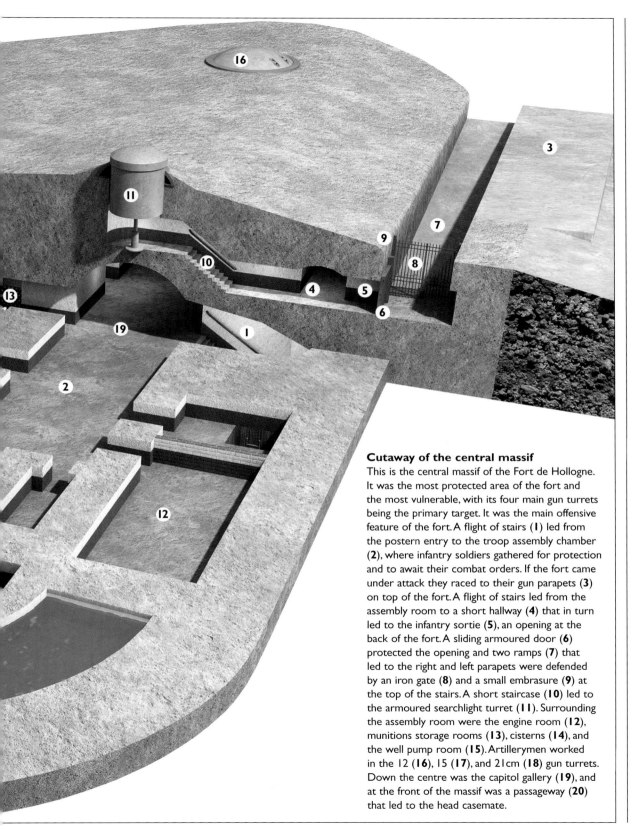

Cutaway of the central massif

This is the central massif of the Fort de Hollogne. It was the most protected area of the fort and the most vulnerable, with its four main gun turrets being the primary target. It was the main offensive feature of the fort. A flight of stairs (1) led from the postern entry to the troop assembly chamber (2), where infantry soldiers gathered for protection and to await their combat orders. If the fort came under attack they raced to their gun parapets (3) on top of the fort. A flight of stairs led from the assembly room to a short hallway (4) that in turn led to the infantry sortie (5), an opening at the back of the fort. A sliding armoured door (6) protected the opening and two ramps (7) that led to the right and left parapets were defended by an iron gate (8) and a small embrasure (9) at the top of the stairs. A short staircase (10) led to the armoured searchlight turret (11). Surrounding the assembly room were the engine room (12), munitions storage rooms (13), cisterns (14), and the well pump room (15). Artillerymen worked in the 12 (16), 15 (17), and 21cm (18) gun turrets. Down the centre was the capitol gallery (19), and at the front of the massif was a passageway (20) that led to the head casemate.

A branching hallway in the gorge front caserne of Fort de Loncin leads up the stairs to the working 5.7cm rapid-fire gun turret, and to the end of the caserne on the left. The door at the far left leads to a barracks room. (Dan McKenzie)

Three-quarters of the way down each corridor a staircase with approximately 45 steps led 10m up to the 5.7cm gun turrets located in the corner angles of the central redoubt. Magazines were located in rooms below each turret.

The central gallery ended at a steep staircase leading up to the central massif, the main combat operations area and the location of the main gun turrets. At the foot of the stairs were three chambers. Two powder magazines approximately 11m long and 6m wide faced each other on either side of the hallway. They were lit by candles kept behind reinforced glass in niches in the wall at the far end of each room. The glass prevented any flames from accidentally coming into contact with the powder. A small antechamber next to the coal-storage room housed the boiler that produced steam to power the motor located in a room directly overhead.

The central staircase leading up into the troop assembly chamber in the central massif. This is at Fort de Hollogne. (Dan McKenzie)

Thirty stairs led up to the troop assembly chamber of the central massif. The assembly room was 20m long and 8m wide. Small rooms and passageways around the perimeter of the assembly room led to the main gun turrets. The motor and generator were located in a room to the left of the stairs. To the right, 18 stairs led up to the infantry exit to the fort and to the searchlight turret. The infantry sortie was secured from the outside by a sliding armoured door. On the outside, to the left and right of this exit door were ramps that led to the infantry parapets surrounding the central massif. These could be secured with iron gates affixed to a large retaining wall opposite the exit. This ramp area was guarded by a small embrasure located at the top of the stairs from the assembly room. All of the original infantry sorties were either destroyed or modified by the Germans.

Returning to the assembly room, access tunnels on either end of the room led to the 12cm gun turrets. The capitol gallery down the centre led to the 15 and 21cm turrets. Each gun turret had its own magazine adjacent to the turret. The turret wells were circular and the walls were made of concrete. The lower levels contained the mechanisms to turn the gun, manually operate the ventilator and hoist shells to the firing chamber. A small steel ladder led to the upper levels of the turret. At the top was the gun chamber itself, a cramped space where the guns were loaded and fired. Gun crews on the different levels communicated with each other through acoustic tubes.

On the outer flank of the central massif were the cisterns. The underground well and the pump room were located at the far end of the cisterns. The depth of the wells averaged 35m. At the far end of the central massif, just beyond the 21cm gun turret was the underground gallery that led to the head casemate. Half-way down this gallery were stairs leading up to additional 5.7cm turrets.

The top of the central massif was solid concrete, very reminiscent of Mougin's 'Fort de l'Avenir', with the steel domes of the gun turrets protruding from the advanced armour collars. A low parapet of earth ran along the sides of the central redoubt parallel to the ditches. The 5.7cm gun turrets could be seen in the corners of the redoubt.

The troop assembly room of Fort de Hollogne. Troops would gather here to await orders to man the parapets on top of the fort to defend against an attack. The door at the left leads to the capitol gallery and the 15 and 21cm guns. The 12cm turret is through the door straight ahead. (Dan McKenzie)

Principles of defence

The forts of the Meuse formed the strong points of the fortified regions of Namur (Région Fortifiée de Namur – RFN) and Liège (RFL). The main line of defence consisted of the new permanent forts manned by artillerymen, engineers, specialists and small infantry units to guard the forts. Field works consisting of gun batteries, trenches, and redoubts supported the main line. One Regular Army division was assigned to guard each position when war broke out.

In his numerous theses on the defence of the state, Brialmont set the following criteria for the main line of defence: it should be far enough away from the city to hinder bombardment – a besieger had to be kept out of artillery range and sight of the city; the distance between the forts should not exceed the average range of their artillery in order to assure mutual support; an enemy should be compelled to attack three adjacent forts together; finally, the fort must command the zone of action of its artillery and, particularly, the intervals between it and its neighbours must be visible in order to view signals and to fire in direct view.

Brialmont was forced to work within the constraints of a wholly inadequate budget. Therefore, from the start, he would not be able to fulfil his own criteria. He had to build the best defensive system possible on broken and hilly terrain. He wasn't able to build the adequate defences needed to secure all of the interval positions, nor did he want to disperse his forces by building permanent interval batteries.

The forts of Namur occupied the highest points along the perimeter of the city. The average distance between them was 4,700m (Forts de Maizeret and de Marchovelette were 6,000m apart), and they averaged about 6km from the city centre. Brialmont alternated large and small forts, with the exception of Maizeret and Marchovelette, which were both small forts.

Each fort was placed near a significant line of communication. Fort de Suarlée covered the Route de Brussels, the Route de Gembloux and the Brussels–Namur

The beautiful city of Namur sits astride the Meuse and Sambre Rivers. The ancient citadel built by Vauban guards the junction of the two rivers. (Library of Congress Prints and Photographs collection)

The Evegnée–Fléron interval

The main line of defence of this right bank position runs along the high points facing the Hervé Plateau to the east. It is easy to see the difficulty of defending the ravines that run close to the forts both in front and to the rear towards Liège. The position includes Fort d'Evegnée to the north and Fort de Fléron to the south. In between are Redoubts 24 and 25, and five trenches. A secondary line of trenches defends the roads into the ravines that lead down to the Meuse Valley. Fort de Fléron also commanded the Aachen railway.

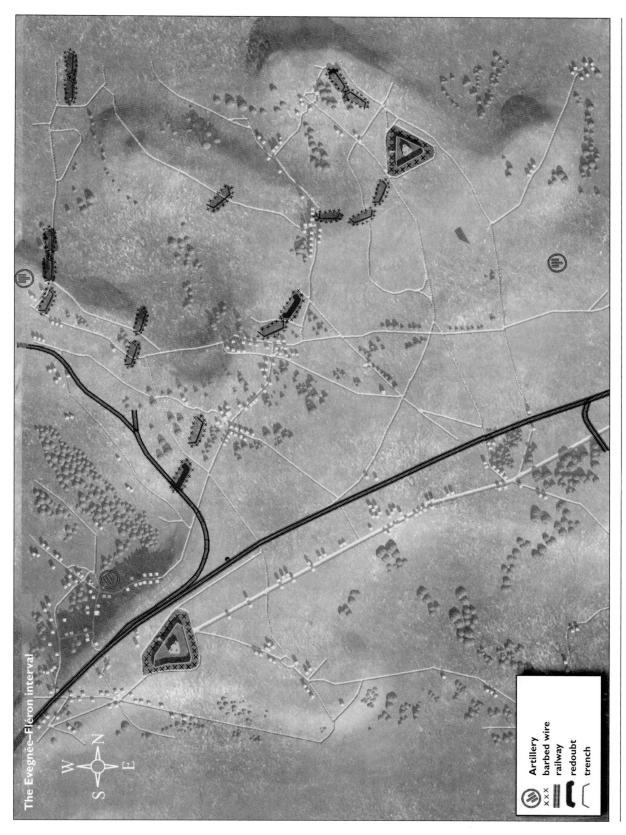

The Evegnée-Fléron interval

W N E S

Artillery
barbed wire
railway
redoubt
trench

railway line. Fort d'Émines flanked the Brussels road and the Brussels–Namur and Tirlemont–Namur railways. Fort de Cognolée defended the Route de Louvain and the Tirlemont railroad. Fort de Marchovelette flanked the Route de Hannut. Fort de Maizeret covered the approaches from the Meuse Valley to the east, the Germans' key line of march that included the Route de Liège, the Namur–Liège railway and the Nameche Bridge. Fort d'Andoy flanked Route de Jaussé and the Namur–Luxembourg railway. Fort de Dave protected the Meuse Valley to the south below Namur, the Route de Dinant, and the railway lines to Dinant and Arlon. Fort de St Héribert flanked Rue St Gérard and the smaller roads leading towards the river from the plateau to the southwest. Fort de Malonne flanked the Sambre River Valley westward, the Rue de Chatelet, and the Charleroi railway. The RFN was broken up into four defence sub-sectors identified in the table that follows.

Fort	Configuration	Elevation (metres)	Distance from adjacent fort (metres, clockwise direction)	Dist from city centre (metres)	Defensive sub-sector
Suarlée	Large triangular	185	4,700	5,100	3
Émines	Small triangular	190	4,150	4,750	3
Cognolée	Large triangular	200	3,375	6,850	4
Marchovelette	Small triangular	195	5,950	6,850	4
Maizeret	Small trapezoidal	190	5,950	8,700	1
Andoy	Large triangular	220	4,100	6,050	1
Dave	Small triangular	190	4,250	5,700	1
St Héribert	Large triangular	245	4,300	6,400	2
Malonne	Small trapezoidal	195	4,000	4,700	2

A diagram of the principal components of a Brialmont fort. (Author's collection)

Fort de Hollogne
Liege, Belgium

Head Casemate
Principal Salient
Salient Angle II
Glacis
Left Lateral
Escarp Slope
Right Lateral
Glacis
Counterscarp Wall
Central Massif
Gorge Caserne
Flanking Casemate
Salient Angle I
Gorge Ditch
Gorge Front Postern Entry
Salient Angle III
Protective Vaults
Counterscarp Postern Entry
Counterscarp Caserne

Brialmont's plans called for the construction of 12 forts around Liège, and one each at Huy and Visé. The fort at Visé would defend the ford of the Meuse at Lixhe on the Dutch border. Huy is located half-way between Liège and Namur and a fort there would restrict a march down the valley. Neither fort was built because of inadequate funding and Brialmont said of this, 'One day we will shed bitter tears over this mortal error.' Indeed, on the first day of fighting, German cavalry crossed at Lixhe against determined but weak resistance. The 34th Brigade soon followed and was able to threaten Liège from the north.

The forts of Liège defended the vast array of communications lines that passed through the city and the Meuse Valley. To the south, Forts de Boncelles and de Flémalle protected the Meuse Valley and the railways running along the valley. Forts de Pontisse and de Barchon protected the valley to the north. Forts d'Embourg and de Chaudfontaine covered the Ourthe and Vesdre Valleys and the railways and roads running along those valleys. Forts de Fléron and d'Evegnée flanked the Plain of Hesbaye, the Aachen railway and the Route de Hervé, the main road into Liège. On the west bank, Forts de Liers, de Lantin, de Loncin and de Hollogne covered the railway lines and roads running to the west towards Brussels. There was no clear pattern of alternating large and small forts at Liège. The RFL was divided into the four sub-sectors identified below.

Fort	Configuration	Elevation (metres)	Distance from adjacent fort (metres, clockwise direction)	Distance from city centre	Defence sub-sector (metres)
Pontisse	Large trapezoidal	130	4,200	7,000	A
Barchon	Large triangular	180	4,200	8,300	A
Evegnée	Small triangular	250	3,100	9,100	B
Fléron	Large triangular	260	3,500	8,100	B
Chaudfontaine	Small trapezoidal	210	4,600	7,000	B
Embourg	Small trapezoidal	190	1,900	7,000	C
Boncelles	Large triangular	210	6,400	8,100	C
Flémalle	Large trapezoidal	180	5,600	9,250	C
Hollogne	Small triangular	180	3,300	8,400	D
Loncin	Large triangular	170	3,100	7,500	D
Lantin	Small triangular	160	3,200	7,250	D
Liers	Small triangular	170	4,000	6,500	D

General Leman designed a defence in depth around Liège that complemented the existing fortifications and was hastily completed under fire. Liège was to be protected by three lines of defence. The first line of redoubts and trenches was 48km in circumference and located just behind the fortress perimeter line. This line consisted of 31 redoubts and 63 trenches. A second line was started 2km to the rear of the forts, 1–1.5km deep, while a third line, consisting of trenches and fortified strongpoints, was located just beyond the outskirts of Liège.

Trenches and redoubts served as infantry positions for rifle and machine-gun fire. Trenches were smaller than redoubts, which were technically lunettes with an open gorge front that provided flanking fire on the laterals and could accommodate a company of infantry. The fields of fire in front of the trenches and redoubts were cleared of obstacles and surrounded by wire entanglements. These interval defences held up well to the initial German attack, but they were eventually overwhelmed or outflanked and the German Army moved into the city.

As war approached railway bridges and tunnels were destroyed or blocked with locomotives, whilst trees and other obstacles were used to block roads. At Liège, the river bridges above and below the city were destroyed, though several were kept intact, and some temporary bridges were built from barges anchored side by side, in order to leave a path of retreat open to the field army, which proved essential in the end.

The central massif of the Fort de Fléron, taken before the war. Early photos of the forts after they were built are extremely rare. (Royal Army Museum in Brussels, Belgium)

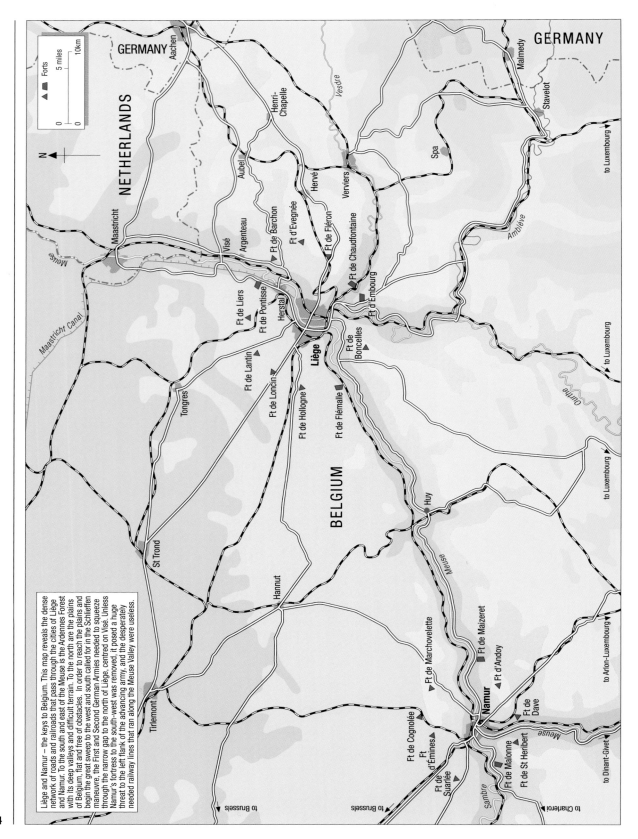

Liège and Namur – the keys to Belgium. This map reveals the dense network of roads and railroads that pass through the cities of Liège and Namur. To the south and east of the Meuse is the Ardennes Forest with its deep valleys and difficult terrain. To the north are the plains of Belgium, flat and free of obstacles. In order to reach the plains and begin the great sweep to the west and south called for in the Schlieffen maneuvre, the First and Second German Armies needed to squeeze through the narrow gap to the north of Liège, centred on Visé. Unless Namur's fortress to the south-west was removed, it posed a huge threat to the left flank of the advancing army, and the desperately needed railway lines that ran along the Meuse Valley were useless.

GERMANY

Aachen

NETHERLANDS

Maastricht

Maastricht Canal

Meuse

Visé

Argenteau

Ft de Barchon

Ft d'Evegnée

Aubel

Henri-Chapelle

Hervé

Verviers

Spa

Malmedy

Stavelot

Vesdre

 Amblève

Ft de Chaudfontaine

Ft de Fléron

Ft d'Embourg

Herstal

Ft de Liers

Ft de Pontisse

Liège

Ft de Lantin

Ft de Loncin

Ft de Boncelles

Ft de Hollogne

Ft de Flémalle

Tongres

St Trond

Hannut

Huy

Meuse

Ourthe

to Luxembourg

to Luxembourg

to Luxembourg

BELGIUM

Tirlemont

to Brussels

to Brussels

to Brussels

Ft de Cognolée

Ft d'Émines

Ft de Suarlée

Ft de Malonne

Ft de St Héribert

Namur

Ft de Marchovelette

Ft d'Andoy

Ft de Maizeret

Ft de Dave

Sambre

Meuse

to Charleroi

to Dinant-Givet

to Arlon-Luxembourg

N

Forts

0   5 miles
0   10km

The gorge front ditch at Fort de Hollogne. To the left is the gorge front caserne and the central redoubt is above. The counterscarp is to the right and the flanking casemate at the end of the ditch. (Author's collection)

Each fort had long-, medium- and short-range artillery, as well as infantry weapons. The maximum range was 8km and the guns could fire all manner of projectiles, mostly anti-personnel shot and shrapnel. The mission of the large-calibre guns was to guard the lines of communication, provide counter-battery fire and to cooperate with the troops in the intervals to defend the terrain between the forts. The targets of the forts were men, equipment and opposing artillery batteries, not fixed, hardened objects.

All of the main guns were packed together in the central massif, an easy target for the enemy artillery. The central massif was visible 1m above the crest of the infantry parapet; consequently, the guns were more exposed than if it were masked. Brialmont believed that destruction of the central massif position would present tremendous problems to any attacker due to the fact that its surface was rounded, which would cause incoming projectiles to ricochet away, whilst the parapet protected the base.

The flanking casemate in Salient Angle III of Fort de Hollogne. The sand-filled vaults absorbed shells from the head casemate to prevent a breach in the rear of the counterscarp. (Author's collection)

The forts of the Meuse were designed to strike the attacker efficiently without being dominated, enfiladed or taken in reverse. Brialmont avoided siting the forts near to ravines or defiles from where they could be easily attacked.

Any enemy advancing under concealment could be engaged with howitzers, which fired in a high, curved trajectory. Plunging fire from the short-range, rapid-fire guns was designed to stop an enemy at close range and provided flanking fire for the ditches in case the enemy penetrated the counterscarp wall and dropped into the ditch. Riflemen in the 5.7cm casemates that flanked the ditches supported the interior defence. The flanking casemates and networks of wire entanglements on the glacis that encircled the ditch offered considerable protection against assault, whilst the second postern entry to the gorge assured further protection if an assailant reached the ditch.

The ditch at the base was called the gorge front, the side ditches laterals. The corners were called salient angles and were named from left to right from the postern entry, Salient II being the

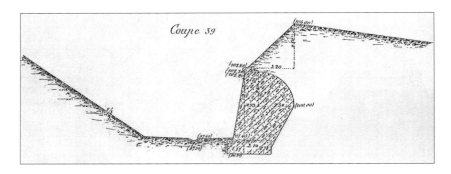

A cutaway of the lateral ditch. The counterscarp wall to the right is nearly 90 degrees while the slope of the escarp rises 2m for every 3m – approximately 14 degrees. The counterscarp wall is heavily reveted to prevent it being blasted away through the glacis to the right. (Association of Fort de Hollogne)

'principal', and therefore most threatened, salient. (In trapezoidal forts, the principal salient depended on which was closest to the front outside the fort.) The width of the ditch varied from 7 to 10m and the depth from 5 to 8m. If an enemy penetrated into the ditch, it was wide enough to allow adequate flanking fire, and the attacker could not fill it in with dirt or debris and climb across it to the escarp. On the other hand, if it was too wide infantry troops behind the central redoubt ramparts could not properly cover the glacis.

Opposite the counterscarp wall was the escarp slope. The escarp on the lateral fronts of the Brialmont forts was a simple earthen slope, covered with acacia thorn bushes or double rows of wire. Some forts had revetments in the escarp, but this was a rare case.

The gorge front ditch was either bastioned or rectilinear. In bastioned gorge fronts, 5.7cm casemates were placed in the flank of the bastion in the escarp. Where the line was rectilinear, the flanking casemate was in the counterscarp.

All of the ditches were defended by 5.7cm flanking casemates. A rapid-fire gun in a casemate in the counterscarp protected the ramp and entry in the rear of the fort across the gorge ditch.

So the enemy could not make a breach in the revetment of the counterscarp of the gorge front, it consisted of vaults filled with earth to take the impact of a shell. This also prevented the guns in the head casemate that fired along the ditch from causing similar damage. Half-columns on either side of the vaults were used to deflect shot into dead angles where the ditch curved at Salient Angles I and III. Brialmont used flanking casemates for the ditches rather than caponiers as they would be better protected from enemy fire and they would be harder to see.

The counterscarp wall was revetted to prevent a breach if the earth of the glacis was blasted away. Shells fired towards the front of the fort could reach the counterscarp caserne but not the gorge face opposite. The concrete of the gorge front was only 1.5m thick for two reasons: firstly it was considered to be relatively safe from enemy bombardment and therefore it did not need the protection of structures that would present a greater target; secondly, if the fort was captured the retreating Belgian Army could shell it from the rear making it untenable for the enemy. The worst thing that could happen would be for an enemy to get into the city through the intervals and shell the gorge front from the rear. Constant fire would eventually degrade the concrete and armour plating covering the windows, allowing shells to explode inside the living quarters, driving the garrison deep inside the fort. This is exactly what happened at Liège and Namur.

Infantry troops made up about 20 per cent of a fort's garrison; the rest consisted of artillerymen, engineers and support personnel. The infantry assigned to each fort patrolled the surrounding area or stood by to make sorties to the top of the fort from the assembly room in the central massif if the fort came under enemy infantry attack. A searchlight in the centre of the fort illuminated the terrain in all directions and a military road surrounded the fort to facilitate surveillance of the exterior.

The living sites

On 3 August, the day after receiving an ultimatum from Germany to let the German Army pass through Belgium unmolested or face severe consequences of conquest and occupation, King Albert I declared to the Belgian people, 'Not since 1830 has a graver situation confronted [our] nation. Long live independent Belgium.' His reply to the ultimatum was 'No'. Baron de Basompierre, Undersecretary of the Belgian Foreign Office, upon receiving the ultimatum and before delivering it to the king, declared, 'If we are to be crushed, let us be crushed gloriously', a sentiment that would be expressed equally by the king and the Belgian people.

Soldiers were called to war in the middle of the night by knocks on the door and the ringing of church bells. They marched with their regiments from the four corners of Belgium, from all walks of life. Units were not segregated based on the language spoken. Names like Damoiseaux and Dejardin share a space with Berwaert and Van Dyck on memorial plaques and cemeteries. As they marched past cheering, flag-waving citizens, they sang patriotic songs and cheered their nation.

Nowhere was activity more frantic than in the vicinity of the 21 Brialmont forts, virtually uninhabited since their construction 23 years before. During that post-construction period, military engineers from the Liège and Namur districts kept the forts in working order. Tests were performed on the guns, on the lighting and electrical systems, water pumps, kitchens and latrines, all with the purpose of improving their function and making necessary repairs should they be required in time of war. On the eve of war, as civilians dug trenches around the cities, the engineers arrived at the forts to put them in order for battle.

On the last day of July the engineer battalions of the Third and Ninth Belgian Armies left their casernes at the Fortress of La Chartreuse to the south-east of Liège and the citadel of Namur. The Motor Pool Sergeant was in charge

Belgian Chasseurs on the march to the front. Jubilant Belgians cheered troops all across the country. (ILN Publishing)

Survivors of the explosion at Fort de Loncin visit the fort in 1923. They are standing in what was left of the troop assembly chamber. (Author's collection)

of the motorcades that would deliver supplies to the forts. These included coal, petrol for lamps, food and utensils for cooking and eating, furniture, uniforms, boots, blankets, lamps, extra wiring and, most important of all, 5.7, 12, 15 and 21cm projectiles and powder sacs for the guns.

Wartime supplies began to arrive at the forts around the beginning of August, ahead of the troops. The quartermaster of each fort supervised the arrival of the supply trucks and horse-drawn carts. Guards at the entry ramp checked the identity of the drivers and the requisition paperwork they carried. Once it was assured they were not German spies, they were sent down the ramp into the gorge ditch to unload. Any available enlisted man helped carry supplies to their various destinations. All of the armoured doors and windows were opened to facilitate supply delivery and to air out the damp interiors that had been closed up since the end of the last summer manoeuvres.

The forts slowly came to life. As troops arrived they reported to their orderly rooms and then paid a visit to the sergeant major who assigned them to their duty positions throughout the fort. Infantry troops received rifles and ammunition from the armoury in the gorge front casern. All troops were given blankets, eating utensils and canteens, and assigned a bed and a work shift. Communications specialists hooked up telephone equipment and strung wire from the forts to their forward observation posts. Telephone and telegraph lines to the fire control posts were tested and repaired where necessary.

The sounds of activity increased hour by hour. On 3 August, the bugle sounded the first reveille at 0500hrs and the first official shifts reported for duty. In the gorge front caserne, orderlies served breakfast to the commander and his staff in the small officers' mess adjacent to the escarp postern entry. Officers talked about their families and mutual acquaintances and speculated about the battle that might or might not be coming in the next few days.

Enlisted troops climbed out of their metal beds in the gorge front casernes. Corporals rounded them up and hurried them to the washrooms and kitchens across the ditch to pick up their breakfast and head quickly to their duty posts. Cooks were busy 24 hours a day preparing meals and wartime rations that would be moved over to the central gallery across the ditch. These included bread, crackers and dried beef to last for 30 days.

Often food supplies did not arrive as scheduled and food collection sometimes required innovation. In a railway station near Fort de Loncin, troops found a parked and unguarded train bound for Germany carrying 12,000kg of potatoes and 3,000kg of vegetables. Trucks were sent from the fort to steal the supplies, under the very noses of the German train crew. At Loncin, leavening to make bread had gone bad so men were sent to 'escort' a local baker to the fort to teach

the cooks how to prepare leaven. The poor man wanted to know how long he would be needed and was told, 'You will leave the fort when my bakers make bread as well as you.' The cooks learned very quickly.

In the counterscarp caserne, the artillery officer met with his engineers to determine the preparedness of the guns and the munitions. Explosives engineers tested the fuses and powder in the small laboratory near the postern entry guardrooms. Troops unloaded carts full of projectiles and silk powder sacs and carried them into the magazines in the central massif. Munitions specialists, wearing soft-soled shoes so as not to create sparks, carefully placed the powder sacs on wooden tables.

Artillery turret commanders and sergeants supervised the inventory and stacking of projectiles in the small rooms at the base of the gun turrets. Inside the turrets, the crews began to drill on loading, signalling, turning the gun turrets and moving the barrels up and down to the proper firing angle. Engineers applied grease to the working parts, scrubbed the inside of the gun barrels, and calibrated the mechanisms of the turret to put them in peak form. Practice drill orders were relayed to the gun commanders from the command post, over and over again until the rustiness of the crews had worn off.

Infantry troops practised sorties through the infantry exit on top of the fort: manning the parapets, setting up machine guns and dragging the mobile

5.7cm guns from garages in the ditch. Infantry teams patrolled the perimeter and the military roads in shifts, as villagers waved and wished them luck and God's protection. Demolition squads were sent out to cut down trees and burn any building or structure within 600m of the fort or that might block the vision of the gun commanders and observers.

In the ditch, tons of coal were offloaded into bins in the storage room beneath the steam engine and dynamo that produced the fort's electricity. The mechanics and electricians, covered in sweat and dirt, worked feverishly to lubricate the engines, load the coal into the steam boiler, adjust water pressure levels and start up the electrical grid. They adjusted screws and belts until the machines were operating at top efficiency. They tested the lighting system and climbed up the staircase at the top of the fort to test the armoured searchlight, making sure the turret moved up and down and the searchlight worked properly. The first night, the searchlights were turned on and their powerful beams raked the skies across the fortress perimeter. Signal teams used the searchlights to test message relays between the forts and to insure sightlines were clear.

When the king refused the German ultimatum, the news quickly reached the forts and they were placed on full war footing. Windows and armoured doors that opened to the ditch were closed and sealed with iron bars and shored up with sandbags. Men guarding the entry to the fort tested the rolling bridge and cleared the embrasures in the flanking casemate. In the command post, the commandant tested the telephone communications with the observatories and the combat positions.

Civilians flee as German troops cross into Belgium. (Library of Congress Prints and Photographs Division)

As the hours ticked closer to war, newfound friends exchanged photos of loved ones. In some places, arguments and fights broke out and the commandant was forced to punish with extra duty or a night in a jail cell. Men sat on their beds or against a wall in the shade, and in quiet isolation, wrote out their wills and last letters to their wives or mothers. The chaplain made his rounds, praying with and encouraging the men.

Commandant Victor Naessens, commander of the Fort de Loncin at Liège, was a man dearly loved by his soldiers. In his memoirs he wrote that their sacrifice and courage exceeded all one could imagine. Naessens commanded 550 artillery and infantry troops during the fighting and firmly communicated to his men that a fort never surrenders, that surrender is dishonourable and that death is preferable to dishonour. 'We struggle, in time of war, to the last', he said. He constantly repeated that the fate of the country could depend on the resistance to the end of a single fort of Liège, particularly Fort de Loncin, since it commanded the railway line to Brussels. His love for his men formed an indelible bond, 'we formed a large family, very united, and we shared a love for Belgium and the King'.

When reports reached the fortress that the Germans had crossed the frontier, Naessens gathered his troops in the gorge ditch. No one who survived the battle would ever forget the scene. After a discussion about patriotism and the struggle to come, Naessens concluded, 'Thus, we swear to struggle to the last shell, to the last bullet, to the last man, and not one of us will surrender.' A unanimous cry rang out: 'We swear, vive la Belgique, vive le Roi, vive le Commandant!' Of the men gathered in that early morning, 300 would die in the days to come.

A small group of Belgian infantry at Namur, waiting for battle. These troops retreated from Namur and in October found themselves behind the Yser River on the only piece of Belgian land remaining. They would hold it to the end of the war. (ILN Publishing)

The sites at war

Lieutenant-General Leman commanded the 3rd Division and the 12 forts at Liège. Lieutenant-General Michel commanded the nine forts at Namur and the soldiers of the 4th Division, who were be supported by a French regiment.

General von Emmich commanded the Army of the Meuse, the vanguard of the German forces, and his mission was to march on Liège and clear the way for the First and Second Armies. The Army of the Meuse was made up of the 34th, 27th, 14th, 11th, 38th, and 43rd Infantry Brigades, plus II Cavalry Corps led by Lieutenant-General von der Marwitz.

Early on 4 August German troops invaded Belgium, with two German cavalry divisions crossing the frontier north of Liège at 0800hrs and heading in the direction of the Meuse River. The German High Command planned to encircle Liège from the north, east and south with von der Marwitz's cavalry completing the investment by circling to the west of Liège to cut the Belgian supply lines from Namur and Brussels.

General von Emmich, commander of the Army of the Meuse that launched the initial attack against Liège. (Author's collection)

The lines of attack were as follows: the 34th Brigade was to march north of Liège to the left bank of the Meuse to attack the intervals between Forts de Liers and de Pontisse; the 14th Brigade was to march on the Evegnée–Fléron interval and the 27th Brigade was to assault Fort d'Evegnée; the 11th Brigade was to march on the Fléron–Chaudfontaine interval; and the 38th and 43rd Brigades were to march on the wooded areas to the south of Liège between the Ourthe and Meuse Rivers in the direction of Fort de Boncelles. An all-out frontal assault on the right bank was to follow.

It was important for the German cavalry to quickly seize Visé, which commanded the passage of the Meuse. Without Visé, it would be impossible to invest Liège or to deploy a cavalry screen on the left bank to mask the main army's movements. At 1300hrs, the 2nd and 4th Cavalry Divisions found the bridges at Visé and Argenteau destroyed. The 2/12th Belgian Regiment under Major Collyns was deployed on the left bank to disrupt any attempted river crossings. The Germans started to build a pontoon bridge and came under heavy fire from Maj. Collyns' regiment across the river, as well as from Fort de Pontisse. German casualties were high. Further north, at Lixhe on the Dutch frontier, two German Hussar regiments forded the river, turned the Belgian left and forced Collyns' regiment to retreat to the vicinity of Herstal. The guns of Fort de Pontisse answered the German bombardment of the retreating Belgians. The guns of Fort de Battice held off von der Marwitz's forces for the rest of the day and he was forced to bivouac for the night without reaching his objective.

As night approached, swarms of Germans advanced towards the forts and the interval positions on the right bank, covered by fire from their 15cm howitzers and 21cm mortars that shelled Forts de Pontisse, de Barchon, d'Evegnée and de Fléron. After a preliminary bombardment across the front on the right bank, the German infantry appeared and advanced in close formation. The guns of the forts, interval artillery, machine guns and rifles fired at the advancing Germans, who

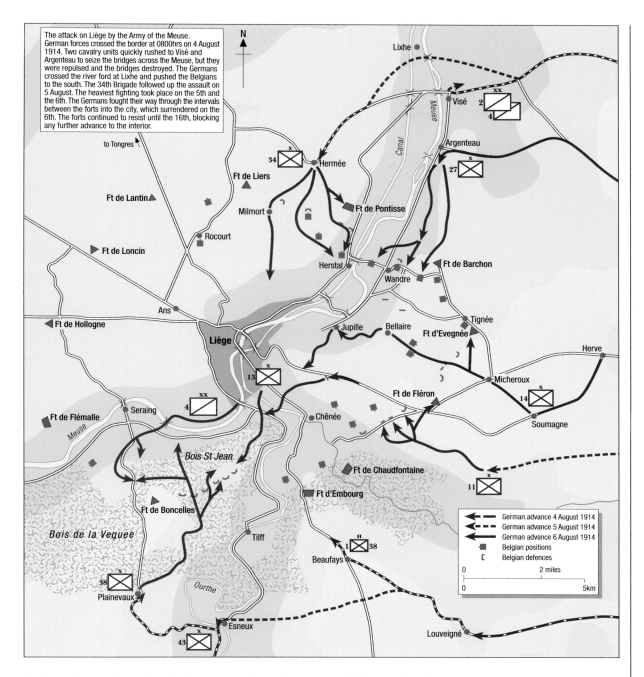

The attack on Liège by the Army of the Meuse. German forces crossed the border at 0800hrs on 4 August 1914. Two cavalry units quickly rushed to Visé and Argenteau to seize the bridges across the Meuse, but they were repulsed and the bridges destroyed. The Germans crossed the river ford at Lixhe and pushed the Belgians to the south. The 34th Brigade followed up the assault on 5 August. The heaviest fighting took place on the 5th and the 6th. The Germans fought their way through the intervals between the forts into the city, which surrendered on the 6th. The forts continued to resist until the 16th, blocking any further advance to the interior.

	German advance 4 August 1914
	German advance 5 August 1914
	German advance 6 August 1914
	Belgian positions
	Belgian defences

kept coming again and again. In some sectors, they succeeded in passing the wire and, despite tremendous losses, reached the trench parapets. The Belgians counterattacked with fixed bayonets and the Germans retreated.

During the night, the fighting continued in a surreal atmosphere. Soldiers clashed under the powerful beams of the fortress searchlights that swept the intervals. The attackers fell by the hundreds with succeeding waves crawling over dead comrades to the trench parapets. A column of Germans advanced in the Faotet ravine near Fort d'Evegnée and was wiped out by the fort's howitzers. Hand-to-hand fighting continued for five hours and those who cleaned up the battlefield the following morning stated that over 10,000 German bodies were removed, a figure that was never officially admitted or confirmed.

Prussian Cuirassiers enter Mouland, near Visé. It was crucial for the cavalry to seize the bridges at Visé and Argenteau. When they arrived the bridges had been destroyed and the cavalry was forced to cross further north. (ILN Publishing)

The following day, 5 August, an artillery duel took place between the forts and the German gun batteries, with German aircraft directing the artillery fire. The fortress guns were very effective, damaging or destroying some German guns, which had little effect on the defences of the forts. Throughout the day von Emmich continued to launch attacks against the intervals, as well as extending his attack further to the south.

Between Forts de Pontisse and de Liers, the 90th Fusilier Regiment attacked the interval trenches, fighting hand-to-hand and with bayonets.

The fighting was atrocious. A German prisoner described the sights he had seen and the 'wholesale slaughter of our men filled me with dread'. They advanced again and again, in close formation. As they moved forward the ranks thinned out more and more and shells burst all around and the Belgians mowed down the men in 'dozens and scores and hundreds'. Heaps of dead and dying lay mixed up together, their cries ignored.

A Belgian officer described an attack on his interval position. The first attack was at night. The Belgians replied sharply with their guns and had no idea of the results until dawn came. They noticed heaps of slain Germans in a semicircle at the foot of the position. The next day, after lines of German infantry advanced they simply 'mowed them down. It was terribly easy', he said, 'and I turned to a brother officer and said "Voila!" They are coming again – in close formation! They must be mad!' The Germans advanced, line after line, almost shoulder to shoulder, until, as they were shot down, the fallen were heaped one on top of the other, 'in an awful barricade of dead and wounded men. It was slaughter, just slaughter!' But the 'wall of dead enabled those wonderful Germans to creep closer, and actually charge up the slope. Of course they got no further than half-way, for our maxims and rifles swept them back.'

Belgian confidence rose as attack after attack was repelled. An example of this confidence is depicted in De Schrÿver's narrative of the fortress troops manning a trench in the Evegnée–Fléron interval position, under the command of Commandant Munaut. He noticed that his men were firing blindly at the advancing Germans, failing to look through the loopholes in the parapets while they fired, and missing their targets that were only 100m away. Munaut also noticed that the German aim was no better and decided to show his men how bad it was. He jumped on to the parapet and took a step towards the enemy – not one single German bullet struck him and the act gave his troops newfound confidence.

The Germans eventually penetrated beyond the trench line, making it to Milmort and Rhee while the Belgian defenders retreated. Heavy, bloody fighting continued through the streets of Herstal and, by the early morning of the 5th, the first of the fortress interval positions had been penetrated and German Chasseurs had reached Liège. Throughout the night of 5–6 August, the Germans penetrated between Barchon and the Meuse, and the Evegnée–Fléron gap, and fought their way into the city.

Once established in the hills overlooking the city, German forces began to bombard the citadel and the city. At 1400hrs, white flags flew from the citadel where a handful of civil defense troops remained. Von Emmich sent a representative to the citadel to accept the surrender of the city but General Leman, who had moved to Fort de Loncin, refused to surrender.

Meanwhile, General Ludendorff's forces occupied key locations in the city, including the bridges. Due to the threat of encirclement, General Leman withdrew the 3rd Division from Liège on the 6th, signalling the end of the ground battle. During the assault on Liège the Army of the Meuse lost 42,712 men without subduing the forts.

The Germans controlled the city but could only move at night and the forts prevented the army from breaking out onto the plains. So far, infantry assaults had failed and the only alternative was to bomb the forts into submission. The Germans were shocked to find that bombardment by regular field artillery had had little effect on the infantry manning the parapets of Fort de Barchon. They simply went underground and waited for the bombardment to cease and for the enemy to attack. The Germans decided to call for their large 28 and 42cm siege artillery.

At 1000hrs on the 8th, 21cm guns were trained on Fort de Barchon. Communication had been cut with the exterior and the observation post of Chesneux had been taken. Barchon's counter battery capacity was blinded. Around noon, the bombardment of Barchon ceased and a German delegation approached the fort under a flag of truce to call for its surrender. Lt. Francisse, infantry commander of the fort, refused. The bombardment resumed at 1300hrs with renewed violence. Shells arrived in salvos of two or four at a time, exploding loudly on the metal and the concrete. The armoured searchlight was struck and immobilized and the barracks in the escarp evacuated because of the gas from the shells that exploded in the exposed rooms and entry gate. During a lull in the shelling, the commander and engineers performed an inspection of the surface that revealed that the cupolas were badly damaged and the concrete of the central massif badly cratered. A shell had exploded in the gun chamber of the 12cm cupola, putting it out of service. The 5.7cm gun of Salient I was also put

A charge by Belgian Lancers against German forces. (Author's collection)

A depiction of the night attack on the fortress line at Liège on 5 August 1914

The armoured searchlight turret at Fort de Loncin. The gallery leading up to the turret is still visible to the left. The turret was upright for some time after the explosion but finally collapsed in the 1920s. The advanced armour rests behind the turret. (Author's collection)

out of action. Had the same team inspected their sister forts a few days later, after the heavy guns arrived, they would have realized that Barchon was in fairly good condition. The bombardment continued with a fury, aimed mainly at the central massif and the rear of the gorge. The air inside became difficult to breathe and the Council of Defence, a group of the fort's officers, decided, with only one dissenter, not to prolong the agony. The white flag went up at 1600hrs signalling the fall of the first fort.

The remaining forts kept up their own bombardment against any enemy forces they spotted. The 38th Brigade was continually harassed by fire from Fort d'Embourg. The advance of the 28th Brigade towards Ayneux and Micheroux was slowed by fire from Forts de Fléron and d'Evegnée. The guns of Fort d'Evegnée successfully destroyed a German munitions column on the military road. Fort de Loncin's guns struck anything that moved on the Plateau of Ans and succeeded in completely blocking any advance along the roads to Brussels and Rocourt. Even a German plane at the airfield of Ans was destroyed on the ground by the guns of Fort de Lantin.

The siege guns arrived on 11 August, although the 42cm guns were not set up and ready to fire until the afternoon of the 12th. For the first time, guns of a larger calibre than Brialmont had counted on were being used against his forts. However, considerable damage had already been done by repeated bombardment from guns of smaller calibre.

The 28cm barrels of the 9th and 4th Artillery Regiments opened fire on Fort d'Evegnée at 0900hrs on 10 August and continued all day long, finally stopping at 0450hrs on the 11th. Shells fell at the rate of 250–75 projectiles per hour. By noon, all of Evegnée's guns were out of service, gas filled the passages, men were suffocating, and everywhere the wounded cried out. At 1530hrs Commandant Genonceau announced that the fort would surrender.

The bombardment of Forts de Pontisse, de Fléron and de Chaudfontaine continued on the morning of the 12th. At Pontisse, unrelenting fire was directed mainly at the gorge front, which visibly crumbled, disturbing the garrison. At

A depiction of the night attack on the fortress line at Liège on 5 August 1914
German troops advance in close battle formation against heavily defended Belgian trenches and redoubts supported by the artillery of the forts. Row after row of Germans were shot down by rifle and machine-gun fire as they reached the wire entanglements. Bodies were piled several deep. On the crest of the hill is one of the forts. Its powerful searchlight illuminates the battlefield for several thousand metres, creating a surreal atmosphere.

The engine room of Fort de Loncin. The motor is on the right and the dynamo on the left. The severe damage caused by the explosion of the magazine on the floor below is evident. This is the only original motor existing in any of the forts. (Author's collection)

1745hrs a huge explosion was heard and felt in the fort. Many thought that the powder magazine had gone up but it was actually the shell of a 42cm gun firing from Mortier. This piece fired two or three shots then retired for the night, leaving the already rattled defenders to wonder what was coming the next day.

Fort de Fléron received 80–100 shots per hour initially, that number eventually rising to 250. At noon, a German delegation arrived but was turned away, though the condition of the fort was not good. Craters 3m deep and 4 to 5m in diameter dotted the earthen part of the massif, while the infantry exit was demolished. The ground around the 5.7cm gun in Salient III was fallen in while the wall of the counterscarp in Salient II was considerably breached. The barracks in the gorge were evacuated and the 12cm gun had been put out of action. In the evening a small cannon was trained on the visors of the cupolas and searchlight, blinding the defenders and allowing a company of the 24th Pioneers to approach the fort. They set up a heavy trench mortar to pound the fort from close range throughout the night. Fort de Chaudfontaine was bombarded from the direction of Chenée from 1200 to 1230hrs by 15 and 28cm guns. This battery took some hits from Fort d'Embourg, which also chased German infantry out of the nearby woods and kept up sustained fire on a mortar battery near Prayon and Trooz. Chaudfontaine took 200–300 shots per hour.

On the left bank, the 11th and 14th Brigades had moved on the fortress line. Fort de Flémalle harassed the Germans in the vicinity of Tilleur and Jemeppe and on the bridge of Val St Lambert. In the evening, fire from the fort scattered a cavalry detachment of 650 men near Neuville-en-Condroz, and a party of pioneers trying to repair the bridge at Engis. A detachment of infantry in the ravine of Gros-Pierre was chased off by fire from Fort de Hollogne while Fort de Loncin did serious damage to infantry troops in the cemetery of Ans, silenced a gun battery near the airfield and cleared an observation post from the steeple of the church of Ans.

At dawn on 13 August the bombardment was renewed against Forts d'Embourg, de Chaudfontaine, de Fléron, de Pontisse, de Liers and de Lantin with a ferocious intensity. New batteries had been installed overnight at Beaufays, Trooz, Belleflamme, Bellaire and in the city of Liège itself. The Germans were anxious to put an end to the resistance.

Fort de Pontisse had been under fire since 11 August and at 0800hrs on the 13th the fire reached a crescendo with the deployment of the German 42cm heavy guns. They turned the surface into rubble, destroying the concrete and steel. Munitions exploded in the central gallery, spreading gas throughout the structure and Capt. Speesen, commandant of Fort de Pontisse, declared that 'Resistance is illusory and the end would come in a matter of minutes', so he raised the white flag. With this capitulation, the 36th Brigade crossed the Meuse at Wandre to attack Fort de Liers from the rear.

At 0730hrs on the 13th an enormous explosion occurred in the magazine of Fort de Chaudfontaine killing 97 men outright and mortally wounding another 30. The fort was unable to offer any further resistance and surrendered. At 1930hrs, after continued bombardment, Fort d'Embourg also gave up the fight.

The bombardment of Fort de Fléron continued with a 42cm gun firing from the plateau of Belleflame, along with other batteries based at Magnée, Micheroux, Rétinne and Liery. Commandant Mozin described the effects of the 42, 'after each shot, the entire fort shook, the shock lifted us off the ground, displacing everything which was not fixed. The asphyxiating [gas] and the flames menaced the artillerymen. Men were burned. All lighting was gone.' By 0900hrs on the 14th more than 4,000 projectiles had been fired at the fort and its surface resembled a lunar landscape, with all the guns out of service. The garrison could barely breathe, and were at the complete mercy of the German 42cm guns. Mozin met with his Council of Defence and decided that it was futile to go on; the fort surrendered at 0945hrs. The fall of Fléron opened the road to Aix-La-Chapelle and reduced the defence of the right bank of the Meuse. Forts de Boncelles, de Liers and de Lantin also fell on the 14th. In all three cases, the cause was unbreathable air.

The fall of the eastern forts allowed the Germans to bring a great deal of artillery to bear on the left bank. Meanwhile, the Belgian Army was firmly dug in on the Gette River and French forces were spotted in the region of Namur–Dinant–Rochefort. The Germans had little time to waste and von Emmich moved everything he could to the left bank.

The guns no longer needed at Fort de Lantin were trained on Fort de Loncin and the bombardment was kept up overnight, picking up intensity at dawn. Shells came from every direction – at times, up to 15 shells landed on the fort at the same time. The armoured plating on the barracks was battered in while numerous breaches were formed in the escarp and counterscarp. However, all the guns worked and kept up a reply throughout the terrible ordeal.

During the bombardment at Fort de Loncin, a shell hit the casemate guarding the counterscarp postern. Munitions caught fire and some exploded and the gun was dislodged. Several soldiers stayed in the casemate to put the gun back in place, despite the danger posed by the munitions. They told Commandant

The ditch of Fort de Fléron after the surrender of the fort. (Centre Liègois d'Histoire et d'Architecture Militaire at Liège, Belgium)

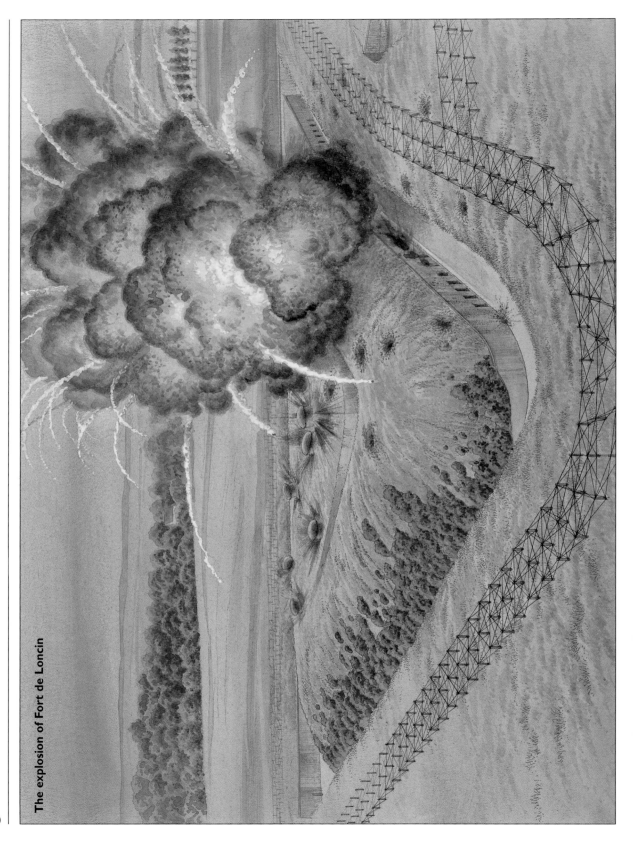

The explosion of Fort de Loncin

A 15cm turret at Fort de Loncin dislodged by the explosion. This is a good example of turret construction. The holes at the top were for ventilation. The steel cap was 24cm thick. (Author's collection)

Naessens, when he asked them if any of them were afraid, that they were only afraid he would think they were afraid. Early in the morning of 15 August, the last day of Fort de Loncin's struggle, the bombardment was terrible. The air was choking and a man could not see 10cm in front of him. Naessens was contacted by telephone by Albrechts, squad leader of a group of soldiers guarding the flanking casemate on the right of the gorge front. It was impossible to breathe, he said, but Naessens asked the men to stay at their post in case of an infantry assault on the ditch. Albrechts replied, 'Then we'll stay.' The men stayed and died of asphyxiation.

At 1720hrs on the 23rd, a 1,600lb 42cm shell fell on the central massif and there was a tremendous explosion that shook the entire fort. The shell had penetrated to the powder magazine, blowing up 24,000lb of powder. A 150-ton concrete block flew into the air and some of the gun turrets popped out like champagne corks, landing upside down on their caps. To the eyes of the German witnesses it appeared that the entire fort had been destroyed and they described it as resembling an alpine landscape. At this point, General Leman walked out of the fort into the open air. He was quite delirious, now a prisoner of war; underneath the rubble, 250 men lay dead.

The only forts left were Hollogne and Flémalle. At 1900hrs, a delegation arrived at Hollogne to discuss the situation with the commandant and offered to take him to Loncin to see the damage caused by the 42cm guns, promising that Hollogne would receive the same if it did not submit. The same message was sent to the commandant of Flémalle. At 0730hrs on 16 August Fort de Hollogne surrendered while Fort de Flémalle gave up at 0930hrs. The battle of Liège was over and operations now shifted to the south-west.

The Second Army was to attack Namur's right wing, the Third Army the left wing. The brunt of the attack was to be carried out by two corps under von Gallwitz – a reserve corps consisting of the 1st and 3rd Reserve Divisions, and XI Corps with the 22nd and 38th Divisions. Joining the attack would be seven

The explosion of Fort de Loncin

Fort de Loncin exploded at 1730hrs on 15 August 1914, killing 250 men under the rubble in the centre of the fort. Turrets popped up in the air like champagne corks, landing upside down. The whole fort shook, concrete cracked and entire rooms lifted into the air and settled down. The sound must have been unearthly.

battalions of cannons and mortars and four batteries of the Austrian Skoda 30.5cm and the Krupp 42cm siege guns, which were to be used to pound the forts. On 20 August the Germans set up the large artillery pieces and targeted the first and fourth sectors. The earlier misadventures at Liège had taught the Germans some valuable lessons and they had decided to attack in specific places rather than across the entire front, and to allow the heavy guns to do most of the damage first. On 18 August, von Gallwitz's forces reached Namur and von Bulow gave the order to attack.

In the first sector, Fort de Maizeret was bombarded from the 21st by the German heavy artillery holding out till the 22nd; Fort d'Andoy held out until the 24th, taking a terrible pounding, while Fort de Dave fell on the 25th. In the second sector Fort de St Héribert fell on the 24th and Fort de Malonne on the 22nd. In the third sector Fort de Suarlée was pounded from the 23rd to the 24th, and Fort d'Émines fell on the 24th. In the fourth sector Forts de Cognolée and de Marchovelette fell on the 23rd.

Over 30,000 shells struck these forts between 21 and 25 August. The interval defences were stiffly manned and put up a brave resistance, but one by one they were outflanked and their troops withdrew, first to the north bank of the Meuse, then away from Namur altogether. Namur resisted from 18 to 25 August and several units of the French Army joined in the defence. On the 17th, the British Expeditionary Force arrived at Mons.

Conclusions concerning the fortresses

The fortresses of Liège were built to withstand 21cm projectiles. From 1888 to 1914 no serious upgrades to the fortresses had been made, including new armaments or reinforcement of the concrete. In the October 1912 Otchakoff Trials against concrete like that used in the forts of the Meuse the following effects were noticed: 15cm shots caused the concrete to shift, affecting the rotation of the turrets; 28cm shots significantly affected and slowed the rotation of turrets. Lt. Gen. Deguise of the Antwerp forts, who observed the Otchakoff Trials, recommended reinforcing the vaulting of the Brialmont forts with a metallic revetment; nothing was done.

The forts were not capable of withstanding attacks from the rear whilst at Liège there were gaps of up to 3,000m in the intervals where the guns could not reach. Some forts were separated by 6,000m and by deep wooded valleys that allowed the enemy to creep up undetected to the glacis of the forts. For counter-battery fire, the large-calibre fortress artillery used observatories only 3,000m in front of the lines of defence. When the observatories fell, the forts were blind. The lack of any armoured observation posts, the naiveté of using telephone lines as a major means of communication and the absence of a liaison between the forts for mutual defence contributed to the problems.

Each fort was equipped with only a single armoured searchlight. If this failed or was put out of action, it shut down night operations. The interval positions did not possess searchlights. There were no electrical communications between the forts.

Signal communications between the forts could only be done with the searchlight, and only at night.

Structurally, no upgrades were done to the forts since they were built. The hygienic condition of the interior of the forts was terrible. General Leman concluded that the main reason for the fall of each fort was asphyxiating gases from the shelling and from human waste.

Conclusions concerning the strategic situation

It is a matter of contention between the parties involved, and historians, if the resistance of Liège, and especially of the forts, had any effect on the German timetable. Estimates range from there being no effect at all according to Ludendorff, which is a ridiculous statement, to a delay of between two and 14 days according to Allied reports. In reality, it is simple to conclude that the delay gave the Allies the opportunity to make some strategic shifts that absolutely affected the outcome and success of the German invasion. Some ideas are outlined below and the reader can make his or her own conclusions.

Crutwell's *A History of the Great War* concludes that the resistance put back the German timetable by 72 hours without which the British Expeditionary Force and French Army might have been destroyed. *La Guerre en Belgique*, written by the Belgian Army staff, reported that the resistance held up 100,000 men in front of Liège and 500,000 men of the First and Second Armies at the border, delaying the German offensive by at least four days. Barbara Tuchman concludes that Liège held up the German offensive for two days because the march of German main armies had not been scheduled to begin until the 15th.

General Normand concluded that the execution of von Emmich's plan was initially delayed by the resistance encountered by the 2nd and 4th Cavalry Divisions at Visé and following that by the defence of Liège; it is difficult to estimate a time frame, but at least two days were lost.

Van der Essen determined that the delay enabled other Belgian forces to concentrate on the line of the Gette. The destruction of pontoon bridges in the north by Fort de Pontisse slowed von Kluck's crossing to the left bank, and Fort de Loncin blocked access to the central plain. In the south, the Second Army marched on Namur via the Meuse Valley capturing Huy and the Liège–Namur railroad. However, the Huy–Namur section was useless without the Huy–Liège leg, which was under the guns of Forts de Boncelles and de Flémalle. In Luxembourg, von Hausen's and Duke Albert's armies advanced toward Namur with the former's mission being to force the passage of the Meuse at Dinant so as to encircle Namur and block the retreat of the garrison. The two armies also had to seize the Verviers–Luxembourg and Liège–Jemelle rail lines and especially Namur–Arlon–Luxembourg, all useless without the capture of Liège. Fort de Loncin prevented the German army from attacking the Belgian Army on the Gette and from attacking northern France. It was not until 18 August that von Kluck's forces met the main Belgian Army. Instead of advancing rapidly, the armies sat on the Meuse for 12 days. The delay permitted the BEF to disembark at Boulogne and concentrate behind Maubeuge on the 14th. Finally, the resistance permitted the French to change their concentration and to move two corps from Second Army plus two divisions from Algiers and Morocco to Mézières and Hirson.

This 21cm turret at Loncin was thrown into the air by the force of the explosion and landed upside down. Note the positioning of the advanced armour in the concrete. The 21cm howitzer is visible in what would have been the roof of the turret cap. (Author's collection)

General Leman writes in his report that, had Liège fallen immediately, the Germans would have continued to march on Brussels on 7 or 8 August. They would have occupied the capital on the 10th or 11th and reached Tournai–Lille on the 13th or 14th. The BEF could not have intervened and the French Army was concentrated in Alsace/Lorraine. The manoeuvre would have been a success. German armies were prepared to march on France at the outset of the campaign and were fully ready by 8 August, the date on which Germany believed Liège would have fallen. But the march on Brussels did not take place until 16 August, thus the resistance of the forts produced a considerable delay in the German march. Instead of entering Brussels on 10/11 August, they entered on the 20th, reaching Mons on the 23rd, which allowed time for the BEF to take up positions there.

Above all, the battle of Liège was a moral victory for Belgium, the Allies and the world. The immediate fall of the fortresses would have produced a disastrous effect on morale of Belgium, whereas if the tiny army of Belgium, ill-prepared for 20th-century warfare, could hold out against the mighty German juggernaut, then the outlook for the French and British was good. The myth of the invincible German army had been shattered and a Cologne newspaper reported at the end of August that 53,000 Germans had been killed at Liège.

The destroyed central massif of Fort de Loncin. On the left is a 12cm turret. In the centre is the 15cm turret and on the left the armoured searchlight. (Author's collection)

Aftermath

After August 1914, for a time, the German Army ignored the forts of Liège and Namur. Trees began to sprout up on the top, weeds grew from the ruined concrete and the structures went unrepaired. From 1915 to 1917, German engineers once again took an interest in the forts to use them in a possible defence of Germany against an invading Allied army. Modifications included:

- strengthening the galleries with steel-reinforced concrete and metal ceilings.
- sealing the windows that opened on the ditch from the scarp and counterscarp chambers
- seplacing damaged or destroyed advanced armour with reinforced concrete
- modernizing the entry to the escarp with a baffle system
- placing latrines in the gorge front caserne
- replacing brick chimneys with cast iron
- building a ventilation tunnel from the scarp, under the ditch, to the counterscarp. Electric fans drew air through an intake vent and provided protection from poison gas and fumes
- replacing steam engines with diesel
- reinforcing gun embrasures with metal.

The threatened invasion never came and, as a result of the armistice in 1918, the Germans evacuated Belgium. For the first time in four years, Belgian troops returned and began to tell stories of the battle that took place there. Heroes were given medals, cowards were courtmartialled and monuments were erected. General Leman spent the remaining years of his life writing his official report on the battle.

After the war, the Belgian High Command inspected the old forts. Although the importance of the forts in the battles for Liège and Namur was appreciated, the fortifications were ignored until 1926 when Belgium once again declared neutrality and decided to build new lines of defence that included the following:

- the fortification of the eastern border from the Netherlands to the Ardennes
- the Fortified Position of Liège (PFL)
- the Fortified Position of Namur (PFN)
- a National Redoubt at Antwerp
- defences along the Albert Canal
- defences along the Meuse–Escaut Canal
- the defence of Brussels
- a bridgehead to protect Gent
- zones of destruction – bridges, tunnels, flood zones, etc.

BOTTOM LEFT The main entry to Fort d'Embourg. Note the modified 'wartime' guardroom on the right, and the original guardroom on the left. This is the only fort of the 21 built in which the entry ramp slopes upwards into the fort. (Author's collection)

BOTTOM RIGHT The air tower at Fort de Barchon. A Belgian modification of the 1930s, the air tower served two primary purposes: to draw in fresh air through a filter at the top of the tower in the event of a gas attack, and to pump fresh air through the fort. It also served as an observation post. (Author's collection)

The Germans modified many of the forts by adding reinforced concrete along the inner walls and a reinforced corrugated roof. This former gorge front postern was changed to a baffle system. The main corridor straight ahead could be closed off with steel rails, moving the entry to the door on the left. (Author's collection)

Position Fortifiée de Liège (PFL)

The PFL consisted of four new, modern forts, Eben Emael, Aubin–Neufchateau, Battice and Tancremont, plus 179 pillboxes, casemates and observation posts built in the intervals. These forts consisted of casemates and blockhouses with machine guns, anti-tank weapons, observation cupolas, and spotlights. Anti-tank ditches and rails, barbed wire entanglements, tetrahedrons, and Contets gates, movable metal gates that could be set up across the road to create a roadblock position, further protected the perimeter of the PFL.

A second line, the PFL 2, comprised 61 interval support posts and eight refurbished Brialmont forts: Barchon, Evegnée, Fléron, Chaudfontaine, Embourg, Boncelles, Flémalle, and Pontisse. Forts de Hollogne and de Liers were used for munitions storage. Fort de Loncin would not be used again for any purpose.

Position Fortifiée de Namur (PFN)

The PFN was of lesser strategic importance than Liège and no new forts were built there. Instead seven Brialmont forts were modernized: Marchovelette, Maizeret, Andoy, Dave, St Héribert, Malonne and Suarlée.

When the Belgian Army began the modernization of the forts in 1929, many of the turrets were found to be re-usable, though just as many had been removed by the Germans in 1918 and had to be rebuilt at the foundries in Liège. 7.5cm cannons replaced 5.7cm gun turrets; Maxim machine guns were used for defence of the ditches and were placed in casemates along with grenade launchers and spotlights. Anti-tank guns were placed outside the forts.

The modernized Brialmont forts became high-tech gun batteries without infantry troops; their task was to provide supporting fire for the field army. New, reinforced concrete galleries were dug out below the original structure. The ventilation and electrical systems were updated, telephone and radio communications installed, and the amenities for the troops improved. All of these modernizations were not only the results of the advancement of technology, but also a reaction to the many problems discovered during the battles of August 1914.

In May 1940, to the shock of the world, arguably the largest and most powerful fortress in the world, Eben Emael, fell to German paratroopers in 48 hours. The PFL fought on for several more days but Belgium quickly surrendered. During the war much of the metal and armaments were removed to build the Atlantic Wall. After the war the forts were sold off or given to historical associations and many were returned to the army. No additional work was ever carried out to repair the damage of May 1940.

The sites today

The military historian or fortification enthusiast who wishes to study the forts of the Meuse won't be disappointed, though many vestiges of the original forts from 1891 are gone forever. There are no remaining gorge caserne entries or infantry sorties as all have been destroyed or modernized. Fort de Loncin, while heavily damaged, is the best example of 1891 architecture since the Germans did not touch it and it still has all of its original guns. A 5.7cm turret in perfect working condition remains and is fired annually on 15 August at 1730hrs to commemorate the fall of the fort. Several other gun turrets are visible, including the collapsed searchlight turret. The searchlight itself and many other artefacts from the fort are visible in the museum by the entrance. The interior of the fort is remarkably well preserved as well. Forts de Hollogne and de Lantin are also in excellent condition and work on their restoration continues. The central massif of Lantin has been restored with false turrets placed on top to show its original appearance.

Many of the ruins are heavily overgrown, several have been transformed by sporting clubs and some at Namur are private hunting grounds. Private companies in the defence industry own two of the forts, and several others belong to private individuals. Three of the forts – Boncelles, Fléron and St Héribert – have been completely buried. The good news is that local historical associations have put incalculable time and money into refurbishing several of the forts and opened them for tours. At Liège, seven forts are open for visits.

Oddly, not a single fort is open as a museum at Namur. During a recent visit to Belgium, the author asked a local group at Namur why this was the case and they were unsure of the answer. However, that should not preclude anyone from visiting Namur in its magnificent setting in the Meuse Valley. And perhaps one day one of the forts will be open, though for now they are private and closely watched.

The bastioned trace of the gorge front at Fort d'Evegnée, now home to the company Forges de Zeebruge. The counterscarp entry is on the left. (Author's collection)

Namur, or in Flemish, Namen, is located approximately 55km south-east of Brussels. The most direct route is along the E411 autoroute. (A short detour takes the traveller to the Napoleonic battlefields of 1815.) The land to the north and west of Namur is a mix of gently rolling hills, small farms and villages. The city of Namur is not visible until one drops into the valley through the ravines that run from the plateau. If approaching from the east along the Meuse Valley, it is highly recommended to take the N90 that runs alongside the river. This road passes by the awesome citadel of Huy and the white cliffs along the Meuse on the outskirts of Namur. The city itself is crowned by the magnificent Vauban citadel overlooking the Sambre and Meuse Rivers.

The forts of Namur are located in a circle around the city. It is best to have a large-scale map – 1:10,000 or 1:20,000 – to see where each fort is located. Fort de Suarlée is about 500m from the N4, just beyond the E42 autoroute exit. The military road is directly across the N4 from its intersection with the N958. The fort sits in the woods behind the Rhisnes Industrial Zone. It is now on private property and in poor condition. The air tower is visible behind the fort. The Brussels–Namur railroad passes close by and drops into an impressive ravine behind the fort where it continues into the city.

What once was a violent war zone now resembles a peaceful park. This is the right lateral ditch at Fort de Loncin, taken from the head casemate. The sloped escarp is to the right. Heavy shell damage is visible to the left. (Author's collection)

Four kilometres to the north-east is Fort d'Émines, adjacent to the N934, just below the village of Émines and south of the E42. It is also on private property and a gate has been built that blocks the military road. Nearly four kilometres further east, on the north side of the E42 autoroute, is Fort de Cognolée while 4km to the south-east is Fort de Marchovelette, still on military land. There is a military cemetery located along the road that joins the villages of Champion and Marchovelette. It is a spectacular and peaceful, quiet site that contains the graves of both German and Belgian soldiers killed in the vicinity in 1914 and 1940.

To get an idea of the nature of the ravines that run from the plateau to the river, drive along the road that leads from the village of Gelbresse to the N80, then down the N992 that runs through the Bois de Hubemont, the scene of heavy fighting in 1914, where the Germans attempted to penetrate the interval between Marchovelette and Maizeret. The ravine offers a beautiful drive with the Abbé Notre Dame du Vivier and the Chateau d'Arenberg as sites well worth seeing. The chateau is used as a training ground for Belgian Army Special Forces. To the right along the N959 is a monument marking the location where King Albert fell to his death while rock climbing in 1934, an event that shocked the nation.

On the opposite bank of the Meuse, near Gawday, a road climbs to the village of Maizeret. Fort de Maizeret is located on a prominent point overlooking the valley. The view from the top of the head casemate is fantastic. The fort is in average condition and is on private land used for hunting. The proprietor's home is directly at the top of the entry ramp, in the former house of the fort's commandant.

Four kilometres to the south-west near Limoy and abutting the Bois de Jeumont is Fort d'Andoy. Today it is also used mainly as a private hunting ground. Along the road to the fort are several interval bunkers built in the 1930s. Andoy is heavily overgrown and the inside is severely damaged. In the woods to the north is the air tower. Fort de Dave is 4km further south and it is owned by the military. Two kilometres north of Fort de Dave is the Musée du Génie (Military Engineering Museum) at Jambes. It is located at the Ferme du Masuage, Chemin du Masuage, Jambes and has some interesting engineering vehicles and a good collection of military artefacts, plus a kind and helpful staff who can give the visitor a good sense of the engineering aspects of the forts.

If you are looking for Fort de St Héribert you won't find it because it has been covered over. The property is now a private farm. Fort de Malonne is 4km to the north in the Bois de Vequée. It is now a refuge for bats and is off limits. This concludes a visit to Namur and it is evident why there is not much to see there

A monument on the road between Wandre and Barchon. The inscription reads: 'On the night of 5–6 August 1914, 500 Belgian soldiers resisted victoriously for one entire night against an assault by two German regiments (6,000 men).' (Author's collection)

in the way of the Brialmont forts, unless you obtain permission from the proper individuals. It is highly recommended that you do so and I would suggest you start with the Musée du Génie.

There are few choices of accommodations in Namur, and there is nothing extravagant. For about 20 pounds per night you can stay at a Formule 1 hotel. In fact there is one located about 1km north of the Fort de Suarlée in the ZI Rhisnes. The Hotel Beauregard is situated along the river below the citadel and looks quite charming. Restaurants are abundant, serving anything from pizza to traditional Belgian fare.

Liège is about 55km north-east of Namur. Take the scenic N90 along the Meuse through Huy where you can stop to visit its remarkable citadel. As you approach Liège you will see the industrial zone beginning near Seraing and Flemalle, especially the Cockerill steel works. Liège also has a number of fine hotels and restaurants. Hotels are located throughout the city. The Holiday Inn is on the river, the Best Western near the Guillemins train station. If you want something less expensive there are some cheaper, but very clean hotels near Alleur and the Hauts Sarts Industrial Park. For a good meal, drive into the city and stroll around the Place St Lambert, Place Cathédrale and the narrow pedestrian streets that run between the Boulevard de la Sauvenière. The most elegant restaurant in Liège is Au Vieux Liège. It is in a building 500 years old in the medieval district near the university.

Seven forts can be visited at Liège, either by calling the association that runs the fort or by checking their annual calendars. The opening dates are different every year. Websites are easy to find by searching the Internet. I have not included any addresses here because they are apt to change quite frequently. Some forts are open monthly from spring to winter, some daily, like Fort de Loncin. Forts de Loncin, de Hollogne, de Flémalle, d'Embourg and de Barchon have museums inside with artefacts, photos and dioramas of the forts.

On the right bank, Fort de Barchon and Fort d'Embourg have regular visit schedules. Fort de Chaudfontaine can be visited by calling the proprietor. You can park your car at the entrance to the fort and walk around the perimeter to see the ditch. It is a very interesting walk and the view from the plateau is excellent. There is also a monument near the entrance.

On the left bank, Fort de Flémalle is open on several weekends throughout the year. Fort de Hollogne and Fort de Lantin are open regularly. The exterior of Fort de Loncin and its wonderful museum can be visited daily from spring to late autumn. The inside tour is not regularly scheduled and you can check at the museum for the dates. Fort de Pontisse was recently purchased privately so it is no longer accessible. A number is posted at the fort's entrance for information. Fort de Liers is off limits but it has a memorial near the original entrance.

Fort de Boncelles and Fort de Fléron are both buried but they are still interesting to visit. Nothing remains of Fléron except for a turret pit. You can still see the postern entry and parts of the central massif and gorge front of Boncelles but the rest is buried. The interiors of both forts are still intact but they can only be reached through the locked air tower tunnels. There is a monument at Fort de Fléron at the location of the former entrance. Apartment buildings now surround the property.

There are some interesting monuments at Liège. On a bend in the road from Herstal to Wandre is a monument to the fighting that took place there on the night of 5 to 6 August. The head casemate of Loncin is now a mausoleum with graves and plaques dedicated to the fort's fallen. Across from Salient I is a large monument designed by Georges Petit and dedicated by King Albert on 15 August 1923. The most memorable of all is Gen. Malleterre's inscription carved into a large stone at the fort's entrance.

A visitor to Liège should not miss the forts built in the 1930s. Fort Eben Emael is about 16km north of Liège along the Albert Canal. Forts Aubin-Neufchateau, Battice and Tancremont are to the east of Liège. All four are open regularly for visits.

A memorial outside Fort de Loncin. It says: 'Passer-by! Go tell Belgium and France, that here, 550 Belgians sacrificed themselves for the defence of liberty and the salvation of the world.' (Author's collection)

61

Further reading

Armée Belge, *Défense de la Position Fortifiée de Namur en Août 1914* Brussels: Ministry of Defence, 1930

Armée Belge, *La Guerre en Belgique* Brussels: Ministry of Defence, 1930

Brialmont, Henri Alexis, *La Défense des Etats* Osnabruck: Biblio Verlag, 1967

Brialmont, Henri Alexis, *La Fortification à Fossés Secs, Premiere Tome* Paris: E. Guyout, 1872

Centennaire des Forts Brialmont à Liège – 1888–1988 Chaudfontaine: Foyer Culturel de Chaudfontaine, 1988

Coenen, Emile, and Vernier, F., *La Position Fortifiée de Liège, Tome 5, Les Forts de la Meuse Modernisés* De Krijger, 2004

Crokaert, Paul, *Brialmont* Brussels: Librairie Dewit, 1928

Crutwell, C.R.M.F., *A History of the Great War, 1914–1918* Chicago: Academy Chicago Publishers, 1991

De Schrÿver, A., *La Bataille de Liège* Liège: H. Vaillant, 1922

De Wilde, Robert, *Mon Journal de Campagne* Paris: Librairie Plon à Paris, 1918

Dejardin, Lt. Gen., *Étude sur l'Importance Stratégique de la Sambre et la Meuse* Paris: Feron & Cie., 1905

Faque, Christian, *Henri Alexis Brialmont, Les Forts de la Meuse – 1887–1891* Namur: Les Amis de la Citadelle de Namur, A.S.B.L., 1987

Gany, Andre, *Construction des Forts de la Meuse de l'Epoque Brialmont (1888–1891)* Liège: Centre Liègois d'Histoire et d'Architecture Militaire (CLHAM)

Hamelius, Paul, *The Siege of Liege* London: T. Werner Laurie Ltd., 1914

Hautecler, Georges, ed., *Le Rapport du Général Leman sur la défense de Liège en Août 1914* Brussels: Palais des Academies, 1960

Horn, Charles F., ed., *Source Records of the Great War, Volume II* Indianapolis: The American Legion, 1930

Normand, Robert, *Défense de Liège, Namur, Anvers* Paris: L. Fournier, 1923

Rhys, Ernest *The Roar of Battle* London, Jarrold & Sons, 1914

Segers, Jean-Louis, *Le Fort de Loncin* Liège: Front de Sauvegarde du Fort de Loncin, 1981

Van der Essen, Leon, *The Invasion and the War in Belgium* London: T. Fisher Unwin, 1917

Viatour, Michel, *Seul Entre Meuse et Ourthe, Le Fort de Boncelles, Août 1914–Mai 1940* Arlon: G. Everling, 1989

Glossary

Advanced armour An outer ring of armour made of cast iron used to provide additional protection for a gun turret.

Arresting fort An isolated fort on a strongpoint of a fortified position with equal protection on all sides, constructed to delay an enemy advance.

Banquette A platform lining a trench or parapet wall on which soldiers can stand to fire a rifle.

Caponier A work built across a ditch, on one or more levels, with rifle embrasures to protect it from an enemy attack, or to serve as a secure passageway.

Casemate (coffre) An armoured compartment for artillery.

Caserne A military barracks containing soldiers' quarters and support facilities.

Counterscarp The inside facing of the outer wall of a ditch.

Ditch A long, narrow excavation of varying length, width and depth, built to deter an attack on the central part of a fort or works.

Escarp The inner wall of a ditch.

Glacis A gentle slope extending from a fortification.

Gorge The rear face of a works.

Lateral The side ditches of a fort.

Lunette A defensive outwork consisting of a salient angle with two flanks and an open gorge

Parapet An earthen embankment to protect soldiers from enemy fire.

Ramp An access road from the military road to the postern entry at the rear of a fort.

Redoubt A protected place of refuge or defence.

Salient The corner angles of a fort.

Terreplain The level ground on top of a fort on which guns are placed.

Turret cap Steel-plated iron covering in the shape of a skullcap that protects the guns inside the gun chamber. The rounded shape deflects enemy shells.

Index

References to illustrations are shown in **bold**